ADVENTURING
through
PAUL'S
EPISTLES

A Bible Handbook on the New Testament Letters

ADVENTURING
through
PAUL'S
EPISTLES

RAY C. STEDMAN

DISCOVERY HOUSE
PUBLISHERS®

Adventuring through Paul's Epistles
© 2009 by Elaine Stedman
All rights reserved.

Discovery House Publishers is affiliated with RBC Ministries, Grand Rapids, Michigan.

Discovery House books are distributed to the trade exclusively by Barbour Publishing, Inc., Uhrichsville, Ohio.

Requests for permission to quote from this book should be directed to Permissions Department: Discovery House Publishers, P.O. Box 3566, Grand Rapids, MI 49501.

Unless otherwise indicated, Scripture quotations are from the HOLY BIBLE: NEW INTERNATIONAL VERSION®. NIV® Copyright © 1973, 1978, 1984 by International Bible Society. Used by permission of Zondervan.

Interior design by Veldheer Creative Services

ISBN: 978-1-57293-312-5

Printed in the United States of America

09 10 11 12 / DPI / 10 9 8 7 6 5 4 3 2 1

CONTENTS

ADVENTURING
through
PAUL'S EPISTLES

CHAPTER ONE

ROMANS *through* PHILEMON: LETTERS *to* *the* CHURCH

THE PURPOSE OF DIVINE REVELATION is nothing less than the transformation of human lives. We should not merely read the Bible. We should experience it—and our contact with it should change our lives. If the Bible isn't changing us, then there is something drastically wrong with the way we are approaching this book.

The Bible is a living book with a living message that God gave us to transform the way we live, and it takes the entire book to do the whole job. The purpose of the Old Testament is to prepare us for truth, and the purpose of the New Testament is to help us realize that truth. In the New Testament, the Gospels and Acts present us with the person and work of Jesus Christ, both in His earthly body and in His body of believers, the church. Following the Gospels and Acts, are the epistles (or letters), which are the explanation of Jesus Christ and the Christian way of living. The letters of Paul, or the Pauline Epistles, are: Romans, 1 and 2 Corinthians, Galatians, Ephesians, Philippians, Colossians, 1 and 2 Thessalonians, 1 and 2 Timothy, Titus, and Philemon. Following them we have what are called the General Epistles: Hebrews, James, 1 and 2 Peter, 1, 2, and 3 John, and Jude. The last book of the Bible, Revelation, is the final chapter of biblical revelation. It is not only the story of the end of history and the culmination of God's plan, but also contains the only letters written to us by our risen Lord—the seven letters to the first century churches.

When we come to the Epistles—which occupy the largest part of the New Testament—we are dealing not with preparation or fulfillment but with experience. These letters of the New Testament are the nuts and bolts of the Christian life. They tell us all that is involved in mastering the mystery of Christ and the Christian life. There are depths and heights in Jesus Christ that no mind can grasp—depths to understanding Him and depths to following Him. Through these letters, written by a number of apostles (though most of them were written by the apostle Paul), the Holy Spirit shows us how to discover and explore the deep truths and the deep experience of knowing and following Jesus Christ.

> Through these letters, the Holy Spirit shows us how to discover and explore the deep truths and the deep experience of knowing and following Jesus Christ.

The epistles are focused around three themes. Romans, 1 and 2 Corinthians, and Galatians deal with the theme "Christ in you." Although that phrase, "Christ in you, the hope of glory," is found in Colossians 1:27, it is really the theme of Romans through Galatians and is the transforming principle of the

Christian life. This is what makes Christians different from all other human beings on earth: Christ lives in us. Paul's first four epistles develop this theme.

Ephesians, Philippians, Colossians, 1 and 2 Thessalonians, 1 and 2 Timothy, Titus, and Philemon gather around the theme "you in Christ"— that is, your life in relationship to the rest of the body of Christ. Here you have the church coming into view—the fact that we no longer live our Christian lives as individuals.

Hebrews, James, 1 and 2 Peter, 1, 2, and 3 John, and Jude focus on the theme of "how to walk by faith." (For in-depth study of this last group, the General Epistles, see the companion volume, *Adventuring Through the General Epistles: A Bible Handbook on the New Testament Letters*, which also includes the book of Revelation.)

This great span of epistles is designed to make all the mighty truths of God available to us in terms of practical experience.

Christ in You – Romans to Galatians

We begin with the first group of Paul's letters—Romans, 1 and 2 Corinthians, and Galatians—which cluster around the theme "Christ in you." Romans is first not because it was written first (it was not), but because it is the great foundational letter of the New Testament. In this book, you find the full sweep of salvation, from beginning to end, in all its fullness. If you want to see what God is doing with you as an individual, and with the human race as a whole, then master the book of Romans.

As you study Romans, you discover that it develops the theme of salvation in three tenses—past, present, and future. Past: I *was* saved when I believed in Jesus; Present: I *am being* saved as the character of Jesus Christ now becomes manifest in my life; Future: I *shall be* saved when at last, in resurrection life, with a glorified body, I stand in the presence of the Son of God and enter into the fullness of the truth of God.

Romans

These three tenses of salvation can be gathered up in three words. *Justification*: I was justified (past tense) when I believed in Jesus Christ. Justification is that righteous standing before God that we receive when Jesus enters our lives—the state of being without spot or blemish, as if we had never sinned.

The second word—present tense—is that much misunderstood word *sanctification*. Oswald Chambers has given us a good definition:

The three tenses of salvation: justification, sanctification, glorification.

"Sanctification is the appearing of the characteristics, the perfections, of the Lord Jesus in terms of your human personality." Sanctification is a process of becoming more and more Christlike.

The third word—future tense—is *glorification*, which is the completion of this transformation when we stand in the presence of Christ in eternity.

1 Corinthians   First Corinthians contrasts carnality and spirituality—living according to the will of the flesh versus living according to the will of the Spirit of God. First, the carnality. If you have read 1 Corinthians, you know what I mean. What a mess! Here were people divided into little factions and cliques, continually at each other's throats, dragging each other before courts of law, gossiping against each other, undermining each other, fighting with one another, and even getting drunk at the Lord's Table! The most shameful forms of immorality were parading themselves in full view of the Corinthian church. Paul, in 1 Corinthians, shows that carnal, unspiritual living is a result of a breakdown in our fellowship with Jesus Christ. In contrast, fellowship with Christ produces spirituality so that we are able to walk in resurrection power and resurrection life.

2 Corinthians   Second Corinthians is the practical demonstration of the Christian's victory under pressure. This is the great epistle of trials and triumphs, of conquering life at its rawest edge. The theme of the letter is stated in 2 Corinthians 2:14:

> *Thanks be to God, who always leads us in triumphal procession in Christ and through us spreads everywhere the fragrance of the knowledge of him.*

Galatians   When he writes to the Galatians, Paul dips his pen not in ink, but in a blue-hot flame—then he jabs us with it to wake us up and stir us to action! This is the "hottest" epistle in the New Testament, because Paul is angry. He is deeply disgusted with the Christians in Galatia, and he doesn't hesitate to say so. Why? Because they are so easily distracted from the truth that they clearly understood and have allowed themselves to be led into a weakening, debilitating doctrine that is sapping their strength and turning them into carnal Christians. The theme of the letter is *freedom*—freedom in Christ, as stated in Galatians 5:1:

> *It is for freedom that Christ has set us free. Stand firm, then, and do not let yourselves be burdened again by a yoke of slavery.*

Galatians is the answer to all the dead legalism that has bound the church in so many times and places over the past two millennia. The flesh, the carnal life, brings guilt, condemnation, and failure. But the Spirit of God brings life and freedom.

I love to read the book of Galatians. As you read it, you see that there is a mighty burning in the heart of the apostle, a flaming passion to see Christians set free of the chains of legalism so they can experience the fullness and richness of the Spirit of God.

All of these books, Romans through Galatians, gather around the theme "Christ in you"—the greatest theme that the human mind has ever contemplated, the theme that demonstrates for us what it means to have the living God, the Creator of the entire universe, living His limitless life in us and through us.

You in Christ – Ephesians to Philemon

The next section of the Pauline Epistles gives a blueprint for living lives that are worthy of the fact that God lives in us. The theme that gathers up this next section is a theme I call "you in Christ."

The whole purpose of revelation, the aim of the entire Bible, is the goal expressed by Paul in Ephesians 4:

> *To prepare God's people for works of service, so that the body of Christ may be built up until we all reach unity in the faith and in the knowledge of the Son of God and become mature, attaining to the whole measure of the fullness of Christ (vv. 12–13).*

God wants us to grow up mature in Christ. He is not interested in forming chapters of the P.W.A.—the Pew-Warmers Association. He wants men and women of action, of commitment, of boldness, of passion, of enthusiasm—a body of believers who will gladly throw their bodies into the battle for His kingdom. He wants men and women who are not afraid of change but who are committed to dynamic growth. Unfortunately, all too many of us seem to think that the theme song of Christianity is "Come Blessing or Woe, Our Status Is Quo." The status quo is the last thing God wants for our lives! That is why He has given us the epistles from Ephesians to Philemon.

> God wants men and women of action, of commitment, of boldness, of passion, of enthusiasm.

This group of epistles sets forth the theme of "you in Christ," which echoes what the Lord Jesus said: "You are in Me, and I am in You" (John 14:20). When we talk about Christ in us, we are talking about the indwelling life—the walk in the Spirit. When we talk about us in Christ, we are speaking of our relationship to the body of Christ—the fact that we are members of His body. Our life is incorporated in the totality of life in the body of Christ.

We are not only Christians individually; we are also Christians corporately. We belong to each other as well as to Christ. By ourselves, we can never come to fulfillment and full development in our Christian lives. We need each other in the body of Christ.

The epistles that comprise the you-in-Christ section are like the books in a doctor's library.

Ephesians   The New Testament book of physiology—the science and study of the human body—is Ephesians, which is a careful study of the nature of the body of Christ.

Philippians   The New Testament book of pathology—the treatment of diseases of the body of Christ—is Philippians. In this letter, Paul takes a practical approach to the problems and diseases that threaten the health of the body. As we read through this book, we see that the maladies that afflicted the first-century church are the same maladies we see in the church today. If you find your spiritual health and well-being disturbed by pressure, discouragement, weariness, and pain, read the epistle to the Philippians for the cure. If you find yourself in conflict with other Christians, or if someone in the church has wounded you in some way, read Philippians. If you find yourself drawn to some new spiritual teaching and you wonder if it is of God—or if it is a deception—study Philippians.

Colossians   The New Testament book of biology—the fundamental study of life itself and what makes the cells of the body function and live—is the book of Colossians. Here we see what powers and energizes the body of Christ and gives it life. We discover the force that binds Christians together.

1 and 2 Thessalonians   The New Testament books of good mental health are the two letters to the Thessalonians. These books show us how to treat depression and despair within the body of Christ. When you (like the Thessalonian Christians) feel troubled and pessimistic about your present circumstances, when you are stricken with grief or fear, turn to Thessalonians. These books look into the future and set forth the certainty of Christ's second coming. Paul wrote these letters to fearful, distressed, depressed people who believed they might have missed Christ's return, who were heartsick over the deaths of loved ones. Paul wanted them to know that when Jesus returned, no believer

would be missed. The entire church would be together with Him.

The key to 1 and 2 Thessalonians is found in 1 Thessalonians 5:23:

> *May God himself, the God of peace, sanctify you through and*
> *through. May your whole spirit, soul and body be kept blameless at*
> *the coming of our Lord Jesus Christ.*

Notice that God wants to give us peace, and He wants us to be whole and faultless in our entire being—not only the body and spirit, but the soul, the psyche, the mental and emotional being. That is the thrust of these two crucial letters of Paul.

In Paul's two letters to Timothy, the young man who had accompanied *1 and 2 Timothy* him on his travels, we have the New Testament book of neurology—the study and science of the nervous system. In the body of Christ, you find certain people who have been specially gifted by God to act as the nerve centers, pathways, and stimulators of the body, carrying the message from the Head to the body. This special gift is suggested in Ephesians 4, where Paul says that Christ has given apostles, prophets, evangelists, and pastor-teachers to the church in order to build up the believers so that they can carry out the work of the ministry. And here is one of those gifts to the church—a young man named Timothy. Paul offers him special instructions about how to stimulate, activate, and mobilize the body, how to instruct its leaders, how to probe and prod and correct and rebuke where need be. The first letter is a message of instruction and encouragement for a young pastor ministering under fire, while the second letter offers specialized instruction in view of growing apostasy and decline in order to keep a church from losing its life and vitality.

In the epistle to Titus, you find a similar discussion of the workings of *Titus* the body. Here, however, the emphasis is not so much on the ministry of the nervous system of the body as on the body itself, on the muscle tone and fitness of the body. You might think of Titus as a book on physical conditioning and general fitness. It shows the kind of disciplined training that the body must be subjected to on a regular basis in order to keep the body in fighting trim. We see this emphasis on discipline and training in the key passage of the book, Titus 2:12–13:

> *[The grace of God] teaches us [some translations say "trains us"] to say*
> *"No" to ungodliness and worldly passions, and to live self-controlled,*
> *upright and godly lives in this present age, while we wait for the*

blessed hope—the glorious appearing of our great God and Savior, Jesus Christ.

Philemon   The concluding letter of Paul is like a physician's book of good nutrition. The body of Christ needs good nutrition in order to live, and the nutrients that we find throughout Paul's epistles—but especially in the letter to Philemon—are love, grace, acceptance, and forgiveness. Without these nutrients, the body of Christ withers and dies.

Philemon, one of the shortest books in the Bible, places a beautiful emphasis on the unity of the body. The thrust of the book concerns a slave, Onesimus, who has run away from Philemon, his master. Onesimus has found Paul in Rome and has been led to Jesus Christ. Now Paul sends Onesimus back to Philemon, urging the man to accept Onesimus back—not as a slave but as a beloved and forgiven brother in Christ. In this epistle, more than any other, we see that the ground is level at the foot of the cross; all distinctions between Christians are done away with in Christ. As Jesus said, there is only one Master, the Lord Jesus, and under His lordship we are all brothers and sisters—equals (see Matt. 23).

This is life and health in the body of Christ. This is what it means to be in Christ and to have Christ living in us. Now, let us open these epistles, one by one, and begin building their rich and powerful truths into our lives.

NOTES

ADVENTURING *through* PAUL'S EPISTLES

CHAPTER TWO

ROMANS: THE MASTER KEY *to* SCRIPTURE

A CHURCH I KNOW OF in Great Falls, Montana was once regarded as the most liberal church in the city. The pastor happened to be in Chicago one weekend, so he decided to visit Moody Church to see what the fundamentalists were saying. He was looking, quite frankly, for something to criticize. There, he listened to Dr. Ironside teaching from the book of Romans. To his amazement, this theologically liberal pastor found his heart gradually being challenged and won over by the message.

After the service, this pastor went forward and talked with Dr. Ironside, who gave him a copy of his lectures on Romans. This man read the book of sermons on the train back to Montana. By the time he reached Great Falls, he was a transformed man. He went into his pulpit and began to proclaim the truths of the book of Romans, and the church was soon transformed. With my own eyes, I saw this church completely changed from a dead, liberal theology to a vibrant evangelical testimony in the space of a few years—and that transformation took place by the power of the book of Romans.

The Power of Romans

The book of Romans was written to the Christians in Rome by the apostle Paul while he was spending a few months in Corinth before going up to Jerusalem to carry the collection of money that had been gathered by the churches of Asia for the needy saints in Jerusalem. We do not know how the church in Rome was founded, though it may have been started by Christians who had been converted at Pentecost and returned to the imperial capital. Paul was writing to them because he had heard of their faith, and he wanted them to be soundly based in the truth.

This letter constitutes a magnificent explanation of the total message of Christianity and offers a panorama of the marvelous plan of God for the redemption of humanity. It contains almost every Christian doctrine in some form, and every Christian teaching is at least mentioned here—which is why I call this book "The Master Key to Scripture." If you really grasp the book of Romans in its totality, you will find yourself at home in any other part of the Scriptures.

An Outline of Romans

In the introduction of the letter, contained in the first seventeen verses, Paul writes about Christ, about the Roman Christians, and about himself. As in every good introduction, he highlights the major themes he is going to deal with, and the letter itself is divided into three major divisions:

Chapters 1 through 8: Doctrinal explanations of what God is doing through the human race and His redemption of our total being: body, soul, and spirit.

Chapters 9 through 11: Paul's illustration of the principles of the first eight chapters, as demonstrated in the life and history of the nation Israel.

Chapters 12 through 16: Practical application of these mighty truths to everyday human situations.

These three divisions grow naturally out of one another, and, taken together, cover all of life. If you will remember this simple outline, you will have a key to the book of Romans.

God's Righteousness Revealed (Romans 1–8)

1.	Introduction	1:1–17
2.	The problem: our guilt before God	1:18–3:20
	A. The guilt of the Gentiles	1:18–32
	B. The guilt of the Jews	2:1–3:8
	C. Conclusion, all are guilty	3:9–20
3.	Justification: covered by God's righteousness	3:21–5:21
4.	Sanctification: God's righteousness demonstrated in our lives	6–8

Lessons in God's Righteousness from the Nation of Israel (Romans 9–11)

5.	Israel's past: chosen by a sovereign God	9:1–29
6.	Israel's present: Israel seeks the "righteousness" of works and rejects the righteousness of Christ	9:30–10:21
7.	Israel's future: the nation will ultimately be restored by God	11

The Nuts and Bolts of Righteousness: Practical Application of the Principles of Romans (Romans 12–16)

8.	Christian duties and responsibilities	12–13
9.	Principles of Christian liberty	14:1–15:13
10.	Conclusion, benediction, personal greetings	15:14–16:27

The Power of the Gospel

This letter is so logically developed that the best way to gain an appreciation of it is to trace Paul's argument, without getting bogged down in details, so that we might see how well the apostle develops his theme. When we are through, we will see how magnificently Paul has captured all the mighty truths of the gospel for us.

To begin with, in chapter 1, we have the central affirmation of the letter to the Romans: the power of the gospel of Jesus Christ:

> *I am not ashamed of the gospel, because it is the power of God for the salvation of everyone who believes: first for the Jew, then for the Gentile (1:16).*

This statement demonstrates Paul's clear understanding of what the gospel truly is: God's dynamic power. After all, who could be ashamed of possessing the infinite power of God, the greatest force in the universe? The powerful gospel of Jesus Christ can change lives, heal relationships, and rescue lives from addiction, depression, desperation, and despair. That is the power of God at work. That is the gospel.

Next, Paul explains the power of the gospel by quoting from Habakkuk as he lays out his core theme in the letter to the Romans: the righteousness of God is revealed in the gospel.

> *In the gospel a righteousness from God is revealed, a righteousness that is by faith from first to last, just as it is written: "The righteous will live by faith" (1:17).*

This is the verse that burned its way into Martin Luther's heart, touching off the Reformation.

The Wrath of God Is Revealed

In the rest of chapter 1, on into chapter 2, and through most of chapter 3, Paul looks at the world around him. He analyzes the state of humankind and sees two apparent divisions of the human race.

Someone has well said, "There are only two classes of people, the righteous and the unrighteous, and the classifying is always done by the righteous." I've seen the truth of that statement in my own backyard. When my children were small, I stepped into the backyard one day and found that someone had taken a piece of chalk and had drawn a line down the center of a panel of the backyard fence. One side of the fence was headed Good People, and the other side, Bad People. Under the heading Bad People were listed the names of the neighbor children. On the other side were the names of my children. It was obvious who had drawn up these classifications: The righteous, of course!

The apostle Paul begins with the Bad People, the unrighteous, the evildoers:

> *The wrath of God is being revealed from heaven against all the godlessness and wickedness of men who suppress the truth by their wickedness (1:18).*

The problem with people is that they have the truth, but they will not look at it; instead, they suppress it. If you want proof of that, I suggest you look at your own life honestly, and perhaps at the lives of those around you. Isn't the power of denial strong in us all? Isn't it true that, if there is an unpleasant or unwelcome truth confronting us, our first impulse is to attack it, argue with it, or simply shove it down into our subconscious minds? This is why people keep so busy in the rat race of life, never wanting to be alone, never wanting to stop and reflect on the deep issues and questions in life. As long as we stay busy, we don't have to face the truth. Suppression of the truth is the central problem of human existence.

> Suppression of the truth is the central problem of human existence.

Because of the suppression of His truth, the wrath of God is continuously pouring out upon humankind. His wrath is described for us as this chapter develops. It turns out not to be lightning bolts from heaven flung at wicked people who step over God's boundary lines. Rather, God is saying to us, "Look, I love you, and because I love you, I don't want you to do certain things that will bring harm, shame, pain, and destruction to you. But I have also given you free will. I will not control your choices. If you insist on doing these harmful, shameful, self-destructive acts, then I won't stop you—but you will have to accept the consequences. You can't choose to live any way you please while avoiding the consequences of that choice."

> You can't choose to live any way you please while avoiding the consequences of that choice.

Three times in this chapter we see how the wrath of God works as Paul repeats the phrase, "God gave them over." The wrath of God results in this condition:

*They have become filled with every kind of wickedness, evil, greed
and depravity. They are full of envy, murder, strife, deceit and malice. They are gossips, slanderers, God-haters, insolent, arrogant and
boastful; they invent ways of doing evil; they disobey their parents;
they are senseless, faithless, heartless, ruthless (1:29–31).*

That is the condition of the rebellious people who display their hostility
toward God and suppress the truth of God by flagrantly disobeying Him,
living without boundaries and doing whatever pleases them. The result is
moral decay and the perversion of the natural drives of life. Even the sexual
drives become perverted, so that men give themselves to men and women
to women, as this chapter describes. This is exactly what is taking place in
our society today—open moral rebellion and open sexual perversion. God
does not hate the people who do such things; He truly loves them—but
He will not remove their free will or the consequences of their actions.

In chapter 2, the apostle turns to the other side, the Good People, the
so-called moral and religious people who are by this time delightedly
pointing the finger at the Bad People who are guilty of so much open and
vile wickedness. Paul says to the righteous people, "Wait a minute! You
Good People don't get off that easy!" He writes:

*You, therefore, have no excuse, you who pass judgment on someone
else, for at whatever point you judge the other, you are condemning
yourself, because you who pass judgment do the same things (2:1).*

Do you see what Paul is doing? He is casting a net that draws us all in—
even you and me! At first, we think Paul is just talking about those Bad
People over there. Then we discover that he is talking about us too. We
may not practice sexual immorality, and we may not be major lawbreakers,
and we may see ourselves as good people—but in the end, we are forced
to admit that we are as guilty as anyone else. No one has any reason to see
himself or herself as more righteous than anyone else.

Those who point the finger at the homosexual or the drug addict must
face the truth about themselves: The sins of so-called Good People are
many, and they include hatred, malice, gossip, slander, deception, pride,
and more. The Good People may be more adept at covering up their sin,
but their hearts, too, are filled with envy, lies, and evil.

Thus, Paul holds up a mirror to each of us—and the image we see is not pleasant. God has judged us all to be equally guilty, apart from His own righteousness.

Next, the Jewish person comes in and says, "What about me? After all, I am a Jew and have certain advantages before God." Paul examines this claim and shows that the Jew is in exactly the situation as the others. Despite being a descendent of Abraham and Jacob, despite being a member of the chosen people, in terms of righteousness, the Jews are no better off than the Gentiles. So Paul's conclusion is that all of humanity, without exception, stands in need of a Redeemer.

> **All of humanity, without exception, stands in need of a Redeemer.**

This dismal diagnosis of the human condition prepares the way for the gospel, as we see in Romans 3:19–20:

> *Now we know that whatever the law says, it says to those who are under the law, so that every mouth may be silenced and the whole world held accountable to God. Therefore no one will be declared righteous in his sight by observing the law; rather, through the law we become conscious of sin.*

The law of God has condemned us all, without exception, because all, without exception, have sinned as Romans 3:23 tells us:

> *For all have sinned and fall short of the glory of God.*

Or, as the J. B. Phillips paraphrase renders it, "All have sinned and missed the beauty of God's plan." We stand condemned according to the law of God, but the grace of God stands ready to rescue us and redeem us!

We see this redemption take form in Romans 4. In fact, Paul outlines three phases of redemption for us: justification, sanctification, and glorification.

Three Phases of Redemption

Beginning in the closing verses of Romans 3 and continuing into Romans 4, Paul illustrates the meaning of justification. He begins by showing us that justification means that God gives us a righteous standing before Him on the basis of the work of Christ. Another One has died in our place. Another One has secured our righteousness. We could never do it ourselves, for we are totally incapable of pleasing God in our own strength.

As a result, righteousness is not something we can earn; it only comes to us as we accept the gift of God in Jesus Christ. That is justification.

Justification

Justification involves the entire human being—body, soul, and spirit. God begins with the spirit, the deepest part of our humanity. There, He implants His Holy Spirit. The Spirit seals our righteous standing before God. Justification is therefore a permanent, unchangeable thing. It is far more than forgiveness of sin, although it includes forgiveness. It is—and this is truly amazing—the condition of standing before God as if we had never sinned at all! It is Christ's righteousness imputed to us—reckoned to your account and to mine. When this takes place we are delivered from the penalty for sin.

Paul illustrates this truth in chapter 4 where he says that both Abraham and David were justified on this basis, the basis of God's free gift of grace, accepted by faith—not on the basis of circumcision or obeying the law or by any of the things people do to please God. No religious hocus-pocus, no striving to obey an unreachable moral standard would be adequate in God's sight. Only God's grace, flowing forth from the cross, is adequate. And God's grace can be appropriated only by faith.

Abraham looked forward and saw the coming of the Messiah (Christ) and believed God; as a result, he was justified by his faith. David, although he was guilty of the sins of adultery and murder, believed God and was justified so that he could sing about the person "to whom God would not impute iniquity." These men are examples from the Old Testament of how God justifies.

Sanctification

Unfortunately, many Christians stop right there. They think that is all salvation is about—a way to escape hell and get to heaven. But there is more to the human life than the spirit, and far more to the Christian life than the salvation of the spirit. We are also made up of a soul and a body—and the soul and body must be delivered also. So, beginning in chapter 5, Paul sets forth God's plan to deliver the soul (that is, the mind, the emotions, and the will).

The soul of humanity, born of Adam, is under the reign of sin. The flesh (if you want to use the biblical term for it) rules us. The life of Adam possesses us, with all its self-centered characteristics. Even though our spirits have been justified, it is quite possible to go on with the soul still under the bondage and reign of sin. Although our destiny is settled in Christ, our experience is still as much under the control of evil as before we were Christians. That is why we often experience up-and-down times with the Lord—sometimes looking to Him as our Savior, living for Him as our

Lord, while at other times slipping back into the terrible bondage of sin.

What is God's solution to this yo-yo existence we find ourselves in? Sanctification.

The word sanctify means to "dedicate to God" or to "set apart for God." It comes from the same root word from which we get the word saint—because a saint is nothing more or less than a person who is dedicated or set apart for God. All genuine Christians, all committed followers of Christ, are saints, sanctified and set apart for His service. God intends to see us not only saved, but free—free from the reign of sin in our lives. Paul outlines the program of sanctification for us in Romans 5. He takes the two basic divisions of humankind—the natural being in Adam and the spiritual being in Christ—and contrasts them.

> God intends to see us not only saved, but free from the reign of sin in our lives.

"Look," he says, "when you were in Adam, before you became a Christian, you acted on the basis of the life that you had inherited from Adam. You did things naturally, and what you did naturally was wrong, it was self-centered. Sin is the natural heritage you have received from your father Adam. But now, when you become a Christian, God does something to that old life. He cuts you off from this life in Adam. You are no longer joined to fallen Adam, but you are joined to a risen Christ, and your life is now linked with him. He wants to express His life through the new you, just as Adam once expressed his life through the old you."

When you learn the process of sanctification, it becomes easier to be good in Christ, just as it was once easier and more natural to be bad in Adam. But it takes time to put our sanctification into practice. You do it feebly at first and you struggle with it. Perhaps it will take you quite a while to really see what Paul is talking about, but when you do, you will discover that where sin once reigned over you, chaining you under the power of death, Christ now reigns over you to life. Right now, in this life, you can experience victory in Christ where once you experienced only defeat in Adam.

Romans 6 begins to show us how to experience victory and sanctification in our everyday lives. Here Paul declares that God, through the death of Jesus, not only died for us, but we also died with Him. His death for us produced our justification; our death with Him produces our sanctification. That is a great truth.

> His death for us produced our justification; our death with Him produces our sanctification.

When God says He set us free from the life of Adam and linked us to the life of Christ, He really did! We don't always feel linked to Him, but feelings are variable and often deceptive. Feelings can be altered by so many factors—circumstances, chemical imbalances in the brain, blood-sugar levels, medications, chronic problems such as clinical depression, or even the weather. Feelings change, but our relationship to Jesus does not change with our moods. When God promises to weld a life to His, it stays welded, and we must believe God's promise, whatever our feelings.

God now empowers us to be as good in Christ as we were once bad in Adam. Day by day, as you come into situations of pressure and temptation, remind yourself that what God says is true and act on it, even though you do not feel like it. In fact, you will probably feel as if this evil within you is very much alive and that it has control over you. The thought will come to you that if you live a sanctified Christian life, you will be missing out, you will be at odds with the world around you, and you will lack satisfaction in life. These are the lies of the flesh. Instead, trust the truth of the Spirit that comes from God.

When pressures and temptations come, whom will you believe? The One who loves you? The One who gave Himself for you? If you believe Him, He will prove that His Word is true in your life, and He will lead you safely to a place of liberty and deliverance.

Romans 7 introduces the issue of our inner struggle, the warfare that goes on between our old Adam nature and our new Christ nature, between the flesh and the spirit. It is a lifelong, frustrating struggle that all Christians experience, as expressed by Paul when he writes:

> *I do not understand what I do. For what I want to do I do not do, but what I hate I do. And if I do what I do not want to do, I agree that the law is good. . . . What a wretched man I am! Who will rescue me from this body of death? (7:15–16, 24).*

You can hear the anguish of Paul's soul as he describes the inner conflict in which he wrestles with himself.

The problem is that we usually try to be good in our own strength—the strength of the flesh. But the flesh is weak and ineffectual against evil and temptation. The flesh is the Adam in us. The best good that the flesh can do is still hopelessly bad in the eyes of God. So what is the solution? Paul shares it with us in the next few verses:

Thanks be to God—through Jesus Christ our Lord!
So then, I myself in my mind am a slave to God's law, but in
the sinful nature a slave to the law of sin.
Therefore, there is now no condemnation for those who are in
Christ Jesus, because through Christ Jesus the law of the Spirit of
life set me free from the law of sin and death. For what the law
was powerless to do in that it was weakened by the sinful nature,
God did by sending his own Son in the likeness of sinful man to be
a sin offering (7:25–8:3).

There is nothing we can do for God, but He intends to do everything through us. When we come to that realization, we come into deliverance. That is when we begin to fully realize what it means to have our minds, emotions, and wills brought under the control of Jesus Christ. That is when we experience the glorious, triumphant power that He has made available to us. That is the process (and it truly is a process, not an instantaneous event!) of the sanctifying of the soul.

> **There is nothing we can do for God, but He intends to do everything through us.**

We have looked at the justification of the spirit and the sanctification of the soul. But what about the body? Romans 8 gives us the answer. Here Paul shows us that while we are still in this life, the body remains unredeemed. But the fact that the spirit has been justified and the soul is being sanctified is a guarantee that God will one day *redeem and glorify the body* as well. When we enter at last into the presence of Christ, we shall stand perfect in body, soul, and spirit before Him. That is the exultant thought that erupts into a great, tremendous anthem of praise at the close of this chapter:

Glorification

> *In all these things we are more than conquerors through him who*
> *loved us. For I am convinced that neither death nor life, neither*
> *angels nor demons, neither the present nor the future, nor any*
> *powers, neither height nor depth, nor anything else in all creation,*
> *will be able to separate us from the love of God that is in Christ*
> *Jesus our Lord (8:37–39).*

God's Sovereignty and Human Freedom

In chapters 9 through 11, Paul answers many of the questions that naturally arise from a careful consideration of his argument in the first eight chapters. In Romans 9, he deals with the issue of God's sovereignty, including the paradoxical fact that human beings have free will at the same time that God in His sovereignty chooses us—what we call election and predestination. We tend to think that God is unfair if He does not choose to save all people, but the fact is that our entire race is already lost in Adam; we have no right to be saved, no right to question God's choices, no rights at all. It is only God's grace that saves us, and we have no right to complain to God that some are saved while others are lost.

> The great spiritual paradox of free will and predestination is that while God has chosen us, we have also chosen Him.

In Romans 10, Paul links the sovereignty of God with the moral responsibility and freedom of man. God chooses, but so do we—and the great spiritual paradox of free will and predestination is that while God has chosen us, we have also chosen Him. All people have the same free will, which operates in harmony with God's sovereignty and predestination in some mysterious way that is beyond our understanding. Salvation is a choice of faith. As Paul observes:

> *The righteousness that is by faith says: "Do not say in your heart, 'Who will ascend into heaven?' " (that is, to bring Christ down) "or 'Who will descend into the deep?' " (that is, to bring Christ up from the dead). But what does it say? "The word is near you; it is in your mouth and in your heart," that is, the word of faith we are proclaiming: That if you confess with your mouth, "Jesus is Lord," and believe in your heart that God raised him from the dead, you will be saved. For it is with your heart that you believe and are justified, and it is with your mouth that you confess and are saved (10:6–10).*

You need not climb up into heaven to bring Christ down or go down into the grave to bring Him up from the dead—which is what you would have to do in order to be saved by your own efforts. It can't be done. The word is already in your mouth that Jesus is Lord; only believe in your heart that God has raised Him from the dead, and you will be saved.

In Romans 11, Paul shows us that even as God set aside Israel for a time, in order that grace might do its work among the Gentiles, so God has completely set aside the flesh, the fallen nature, so that we might learn what God will do for us and through us. When we freely admit that without Christ we can do nothing—and when we live our lives accordingly, totally dependent upon Him—then we discover that we can do all things through Him who strengthens us (see Phil. 4:13). And what an amazing discovery that is!

Pride, therefore, is our greatest temptation and our cruelest enemy. Someday, even our flesh will serve God by His grace—our glorified flesh. In the day when creation is freed from its bondage to sin and the sons of God stand forth in resurrection bodies, then even that which was once rejected and cursed shall demonstrate the power and wisdom of God.

A Living Sacrifice

The final section of Romans, chapters 12 through 16, begins with these words:

> *I urge you, brothers, in view of God's mercy, to offer your bodies as living sacrifices, holy and pleasing to God—this is your spiritual [or reasonable] act of worship (12:1).*

The most reasonable, intelligent, thoughtful, purposeful, spiritual thing you can do with your life, in view of all these great facts that Paul has declared to you, is to give yourself to God and to live for Him. Nothing else can fulfill you to any degree. Therefore, give yourself to Him as a living sacrifice. It's the only reasonable thing to do!

How do we do that? How do we offer our bodies as living sacrifices to God? That's what the rest of Romans is about: Practical application of these truths in our everyday lives. When you follow these principles, you will find your life being changed in all your relationships. First, it is changed with regard to your Christian brothers and sisters, as Romans 12:3–13 shows. Presenting your body as a living sacrifice affects your life in the church.

Next, as we see in Romans 12:14 through the end of chapter 13, Paul shows how this way of life affects our relationships to the governing powers and to society in general. Even your inner attitudes will be different, as Paul explains in Romans 14 and 15. Your attitudes toward those who disagree with you and hold different values than you will be changed. Also, your attitude toward the lost will be transformed. You will feel a burning passion to reach those who are lost and live apart from Christ.

There is no more powerful way to close this brief survey of the letter that offers us the master key to Scripture than with the same words Paul uses to conclude this powerful epistle, Romans 16:25–27:

> *Now to him who is able to establish you by my gospel and the proclamation of Jesus Christ, according to the revelation of the mystery hidden for long ages past, but now revealed and made known through the prophetic writings by the command of the eternal God, so that all nations might believe and obey him—to the only wise God be glory forever through Jesus Christ!*

NOTES

NOTES

NOTES

ADVENTURING
through
PAUL'S EPISTLES

CHAPTER THREE

1 CORINTHIANS:
THE EPISTLE
to the
21ST CENTURY

OURS IS A SOCIETY DEVOTED to sensualism and pleasure, where nothing seems too extreme to be censored or forbidden. It is also an information-oriented society, devoted to the rapid transmission and endless analysis of events, ideas, and philosophies. We are living in a postmodern, post-Christian age—an age of tabloid TV, incessant talk shows, rampant prostitution, adultery, homosexuality, pornography, and child pornography.

In the midst of all this, Paul's first epistle to the Corinthians is extremely relevant because it so thoroughly captures the problems that we face as Christians in this culture. And of all the first-century cities we find in the New Testament, Corinth most closely resembles American culture today.

> Of all the first-century cities in the New Testament, Corinth most closely resembles American culture today.

Corinth was a resort city, the capital of pleasure-seeking in the first century world. Located on the Peloponnesian peninsula, it was a beautiful city of palms and magnificent buildings. It also drew the great thinkers and speakers of Greece. They would gather in the public forums and talk endlessly about ideas and issues—from politics to philosophy, from economics to metaphysics, from entertainment to morality. These were the low-tech forerunners of our mass-media public forums today. The city of Corinth was the cultural heir of the great thinkers of the Golden Age of Greece; Socrates, Plato, and Aristotle all had their devoted followers within the city of Corinth.

Corinth was also devoted to the worship of the goddess of sex. In the city there was a temple dedicated to the Greek goddess of love, Aphrodite, and part of the goddess worship was the performance of certain religious ceremonies involving sexual activity. The priestesses of this temple were actually prostitutes, and some ten thousand of them served in the temple. The city was openly given over to the most depraved forms of sexual activity, and then—as now—unrestrained sensualism and obscenity were not only tolerated, but approved by the leaders and opinion-makers of society.

Paul in Corinth

Into this city came the apostle Paul. You remember the story from the book of Acts. Paul had come down through Thessalonica and had been driven out of that city by an uprising of the Jews against him. From there he passed briefly through the little city of Berea and then went down into Athens. Walking through Athens, he noted the many temples to various pagan gods, and he went to preach to the Athenians on Mars Hill. When he left Athens, he traveled across the little isthmus into Corinth, where he stayed for about a year and a half to two years, preaching the gospel and making tents for a living.

In Corinth, Paul met Aquila and Priscilla, a couple who had come from Rome and who were also tentmakers. He stayed with them and led them to Christ. He then formed a church in their home and the gospel spread throughout the city from that first Corinthian church. Many Corinthians, on hearing the gospel, believed and were baptized and became members of this church.

This was the church to which Paul wrote his letter. And as you read it, you will see that the Corinthian church was a problem-plagued church—probably the greatest problem church in the New Testament! Yet the Corinthian church also had much to commend it. As Paul begins his letter to them, he affirms this, reminding them of their calling to be sanctified and holy, set apart for God's service:

> *To the church of God in Corinth, to those sanctified in Christ Jesus and called to be holy, together with all those everywhere who call on the name of our Lord Jesus Christ—their Lord and ours:*
> *Grace and peace to you from God our Father and the Lord Jesus Christ (1 Cor. 1:2–3).*

He goes on to tell why the Corinthian believers are what they are: followers of the Lord Jesus Christ. He writes about the great themes of the Christian faith, which the Corinthians have believed and put into practice. He notes that they have received Christ by faith and by grace, and so they have entered into a new life.

Then Paul comes to this key statement—the statement around which every other point in this letter is built:

> *God, who has called you into fellowship with his Son Jesus Christ our Lord, is faithful (1:9).*

This is the central truth of the Christian life: We are called to share the life of the Son of God. Everything that follows in this letter focuses around this verse and this concept of sharing and fellowship with Jesus.

> "This is the central truth of the Christian life: We are called to share the life of the Son of God."

The Outline of 1 Corinthians

The letter to the Corinthians falls into two major divisions: chapters 1 through 11 deal with what we might call "the carnalities," and chapters 12 through 16 focus on what Paul calls "the spiritualities." The carnalities include everything that is wrong with the Corinthian church. The spiritualities include everything the church needs to do to correct what is wrong.

The Carnalities—What Is Wrong (1 Corinthians 1–11)

1.	Introduction	1:1–9
2.	Paul addresses the issue of division in the church	1:10–4:21
3.	Paul addresses the issue of sexual immorality	5
4.	Paul addresses litigation between Christians	6:1–11
5.	Paul warns against sexual immorality	6:12–20
6.	Paul answers questions from the Corinthian church	7–11
	A. Counsel on marriage	7
	B. Christian liberty and the weaker Christian	8:1–11:1
	C. On public prayer	11:2–16
	D. Disorder at the Lord's Table	11:17–34

The Spiritualities—How to Correct What Is Wrong (1 Corinthians 12–16)

7.	Spiritual gifts	12–14
8.	Applying the reality of the resurrection of Jesus Christ to our everyday lives	15
9.	Collecting for the needy	16:1–4
10.	Conclusion	16:5–24

As you read this letter, you will see not only the problems of the Corinthian church but you will also recognize the problems of the church in America today. Like the first-century Corinthians, we suffer from all the carnalities—at least in principle. And in order to set our lives straight, we need the spiritualities. First Corinthians is directed to believers living in a sex-saturated atmosphere, dominated by the constant ebb and flow of ideas and information. It is directed to Christians who are living in the midst of pressures and temptations of the kind you and I face every day.

In the first section, Paul identifies and addresses three major problem areas in this church: First, there is the problem of divisions within the church; second, there is the problem of scandals in the church; and third, he takes up certain questions that the Corinthian Christians have asked him about.

The Carnalities—What Is Wrong with the Corinthian Church

The first problem—divisions within the church—is the result of the surrounding culture infecting the church. And this is a problem we contend with today. You hear it again and again: "The church is lagging behind! The church is out of step! We need to catch up with the times in which we live!" While I would never want the church to be stodgy and resistant to change, I would be even more horrified to see the church become indistinguishable from the world around us! When a church begins to reflect the spirit of the age in which it lives, it ceases to reflect Jesus Christ; it ceases to be sanctified, set apart, and distinct from the culture. When that happens, the church loses its power—and that is what had happened to the church at Corinth.

The Corinthian Christians had allowed divisions over human philosophies to come into the church. They had chosen to gather around certain religious leaders, and now they were divided into factions, saying, "I follow so-and-so, and his insights are better and truer than the foolishness you and your leader believe!" Sects, factions, and cliques had arisen so that some were following Peter, some Apollos, and some were gathering about the teachings of Paul himself. There was even an exclusive little group that claimed to be the purest of all—they said they followed Christ alone! And they were the worst troublemakers of all because of their spiritual pride!

Healing the Divisions

Paul begins to address this by showing that human wisdom is useless. He sets it aside completely and says that human insights are always partial and untrustworthy to a great degree. The Corinthians will never learn anything, he insists, until they give themselves to the wisdom of God.

> *For since in the wisdom of God the world through its wisdom did not know him, God was pleased through the foolishness of what was preached to save those who believe (1:21).*

The deep issues of God and the life of the spirit cannot be settled by a popularity contest or by philosophical debate. They can only be settled by the Word of God.

> *The deep issues of God and the life of the spirit can only be settled by the Word of God.*

The church, then or now, will never solve its problems as long as it pursues this writer and that teacher, this pastor or that speaker. Insight comes from the Spirit of God, speaking to us through His Word.

I would be horrified if you were to read this book and then go around quoting Ray Stedman, holding me up as some great authority. This book is intended to be a guide, a kind of road map in your own personal study of God's Word. If you emerge from our adventure together through the Bible better equipped to go out and say, "This is what the Bible says about that," then I will be pleased; I will feel I have done my job.

The apostle Paul answers the factions and divisions in Corinth by confronting the Corinthian church with the word of the cross—the word that presents the cross of Christ as the instrument by which God cuts off all human wisdom, not as being worthless in its own narrow realm, but as being useless in solving the major problems of human beings. Paul writes,

> *The message [or word] of the cross is foolishness to those who are perishing, but to us who are being saved it is the power of God (1:18).*

When we understand this, we realize that we will never begin to learn until we first learn that we do not know anything. When we come to appreciate the word of the cross, we understand that God took His own Son, a completely perfect human being, made like us in every way, and nailed Him up to die. That is the word of the cross. That is why the cross looks so foolish to the natural man and woman.

The cross of Christ operates on a totally different principle than worldly wisdom. It is like a saw that rips across the grain of the wisdom of this world. Once we understand and accept that fact, says Paul, we begin to discover the true, secret, hidden wisdom that unwraps the problems of life and answers them, one by one. We begin to understand ourselves and to see why this world is the way it is and where it is heading and why all the confusion and problems of life exist.

Paul is saying, in effect, "I'm not going to waste time arguing with you about the philosophies of Socrates or Plato or Aristotle or the wisdom of any other human being. They have their place. But when it comes to solving the deep-seated problems of human nature, there is only one wisdom that can touch it, and that is the word of the cross."

This is one of the mightiest answers of all time to the intellectualism that constantly hounds the Christian church and attempts to undermine it. God designed us to learn, inquire, and wonder, but He never intended that all our knowledge should come from worldly sources. He designed us to learn from Him, to seek our answers from Him. And He provided the answers in the form of revelation in Scripture. Our knowledge must have a right foundation, so He constantly calls us back to the principle He laid down in the Old Testament:

The fear of the LORD is the beginning of wisdom, and knowledge of the Holy One is understanding (Prov. 9:10).

The True Source of Knowledge and Wisdom

That is the true source of knowledge and wisdom. That is where we must begin.

The cause of the divisions in the Corinthian church was not differences of human points of view. No, you can have many points of view on many issues in a church and still have unity and fellowship. The cause of their divisions was carnality, pride, and the fleshly desire to have preeminence and to be idolized and praised. Paul tells them that while carnality is at work in their lives, they will remain spiritual infants. They will never grow.

> "The cause of division was carnality, pride, and the fleshly desire to have preeminence and to be idolized and praised.

All that we do in the flesh is wood, hay, and stubble, fit only to be burned. All the praise we crave and seek from others is worthless—no, worse than worthless, for when we crave it and seek it, we bring division and destruction to God's work. God's judgment is true and it is relentless; He is not the least bit impressed by the works we do in the flesh. Only what is done in the Spirit will last. The word of the cross must come in and cut off the flesh before we can experience growth and maturity. Until that happens, division and conflict will reign in the church and in our lives.

Next, Paul turns to the matter of the scandals in this church. These were, of course, also the result of the carnality of the Corinthian church.

Dealing with the Scandals

Paul bluntly acknowledges the sexual immorality in the church and cites a specific case—a case that was being openly regarded with acceptance and tolerance. Paul's response? This sin must be dealt with! Whenever sin breaks out openly and there is no repentance, the church must act in discipline—yet the Corinthian church had failed to act! As a result, immorality was eating away at the ranks of the Corinthian church.

Here again we see a parallel to the church today. It is frightening to see certain leaders of the church openly advocating sexual immorality, encouraging young people to sleep together and live together, and even commending people for the ministry who are living openly immoral relationships. Today, as in first-century Corinth, we are surrounded by a culture that accepts immorality as normal, even healthy. But we in the church must stand for the fact that the violation of God's laws of sexual conduct are, in fact, a violation of the humanity of the individuals involved.

It is not just the wrath of God that burns when there is sexual sin; it is truly the love of God that burns. God loves us too much to allow us to hurt ourselves and each other by abusing one another sexually, joining ourselves body and soul to those with whom we have no lifelong, God-honored relationship, and using each other for self-gratification rather than honoring one another other as brothers and sisters in Christ. It is not only God's law but God's love for us that is transgressed when we sin sexually against one another.

If we want young people to keep themselves sexually pure, we must help them to understand that sex is more than just a matter of "thou shalt not." They need to understand that their bodies are the temples of the Holy Spirit. The Son of God Himself dwells in us, and we are never out of His presence. Everywhere we go, He goes with us and is in us. Everything we do is done in the presence of the Son of God Himself. Would we drag Jesus into a house of prostitution, into the presence of pornography, or into the backseat of a car? What a horrible thought! If our young people can learn to practice His presence and to consciously take Him wherever they go, they will be better equipped to withstand the pressures and temptations that come their way.

Answering Their Questions

Beginning with chapter 7, Paul turns to the four major questions the Corinthians had written to him about—marriage, meat that had been offered to idols, women's hats, and the Lord's Table.

Marriage First, the Corinthians had asked Paul if it was right to be married, in view of the pressures that surrounded them. They wondered if, perhaps, they should give themselves completely to the service of God in an ascetic lifestyle. Although Paul himself was not married, he told them that it is best, if possible, for men and women to be married, and that marriage is a perfectly proper way of life. Each man should have his own wife and each woman her own husband.

Then he went on to say that it is also right to have a single life if God grants this as a special calling to any individual. Singleness, too, is a perfectly honorable way of life. Marriage is not a necessity, though it is often an advantage. But marriage can also be a problem. Paul deals thoughtfully, helpfully, and carefully with this whole question of marriage.

Second, the Corinthians had written Paul about meat that had been offered to idols. They were worried about offending God and about offending the conscience of the weaker Christian in this matter. Although we are no longer troubled by the problem of whether we ought to eat meat offered to idols or not, we are still confronting this same principle. We have Christian taboos about many issues that are not directly addressed or stated to be evil in Scripture: smoking, social drinking, dancing, and many other issues. Meat Offered to Idols

It is interesting that Paul was an apostle, with all the authority of an apostle, but he absolutely refused to make up any rules about these matters. Why? Because weak, immature Christians always want somebody to put them under law. But if you put Christians under law, then they are no longer under grace, and Paul knew that Christians must learn to deal with what he calls "the law of liberty."

Instead, he links "the law of liberty" with two other laws. One he calls the "law of love": that is, the law that says, "I may be free to do it, but if I am really putting a stumbling block in somebody else's path, I won't do it." This limitation is not imposed by my conscience but by another's conscience—and by my Christian love for that person. I set aside my rights in order to avoid offending the person whose conscience is more legalistic or fragile.

The other law Paul appeals to is the "law of expediency": that is, everything is legal and lawful, but not everything is helpful or expedient. There are a lot of things I could do, and many directions I could go as a Christian, but if I spend all my time doing all the things I am free to do, I no longer have any time to do the things I am called to do. That is not helpful or expedient.

Third, the Corinthians had asked Paul about a problem with women's hats. Hats? Yes, hats! It may sound silly today in our culture, but it was a big issue in that time and place—and not as silly as you might think. This particular church had a problem because of the local culture. If a woman was seen bareheaded in Corinth, she was immediately identified Women's Hats as a prostitute, one of the temple priestesses, and that is why Paul writes to these people in Corinth and says, "You women, when you come to church, put a hat on! It is a sign that you are a Christian woman subject to your husband" (my paraphrase; see 1 Cor. 11:3–16).

The Lord's Table The fourth problem the Corinthians asked about concerned the Lord's Table. There were certain ones in the church who were partaking of the Lord's Supper in a mechanical way, seeing no meaning and having no insight into what they were doing. So the apostle had to show them that everything the Christian does must be done realistically, with a clear understanding of the meaning of the Lord's Supper and with a recognition that it must be done as to the Lord.

Correcting the Carnalities

In chapter 12 and throughout the rest of the book, Paul deals with the great spiritualities, which are the correction to these carnalities. These problems could not be corrected by human effort. Any correction must begin with recognition of the ministry of the Holy Spirit in the believer's life. Notice that chapter 12 begins with that very word, *spiritualities*:

> *Now about spiritual gifts, brothers, I do not want you to be ignorant (12:1).*

The English translation here uses two words, "spiritual gifts," but in the original Greek language there is only one word here, and it is a word that might most literally be interpreted "spiritualities."

Paul says he does not want the Corinthians to be uninformed concerning the spiritualities. Why not? Well, because the spiritual realm, even though invisible, is the realm of ultimate reality. The spiritualities make all other realms of life work. It is the presence of the Spirit that makes Christ real to us, and the gifts of the Spirit—the spiritualities—are designed to make the body of Christ function effectively and in a healthy way. As the church performs its function, it reaches out and affects society on every side, carrying out the eternal plan of God.

We have missed so much of the great richness of the provision of Christ for His church. We know so little about the gifts of the Spirit. What is your gift? Do you know? Have you discovered it? Are you using it? Or do you need the same spiritual prodding that Paul gave Timothy:

For this reason I remind you to fan into flame the gift of God,
which is in you through the laying on of my hands (2 Tim. 1:6).

The body of Christ functions by the exercise of its gifts, and every Christian has at least one gift. There are many different gifts, and we do not all have the same gift. That's why we need each other in the body of Christ: No two Christians are alike, and no one Christian is expendable. If one Christian fails to exercise his or her gifts, the entire body of Christ suffers.

Chapter 12 is a beautiful chapter, clearly showing us that we must not despise or offend one another because of a difference in gifts. One of the most beautiful—and convicting—passages in this chapter is the passage that clearly defines the church as a body made up of many indispensable parts:

> *God has arranged the parts in the body, every one of them, just as he wanted them to be. If they were all one part, where would the body be? As it is, there are many parts, but one body.*
> *The eye cannot say to the hand, "I don't need you!" And the head cannot say to the feet, "I don't need you!" On the contrary, those parts of the body that seem to be weaker are indispensable, and the parts that we think are less honorable we treat with special honor. And the parts that are unpresentable are treated with special modesty, while our presentable parts need no special treatment. But God has combined the members of the body and has given greater honor to the parts that lacked it, so that there should be no division in the body, but that its parts should have equal concern for each other (1 Cor. 12:18–25).*

As we live in unity, carrying out our functions in the church and in the world by exercising our spiritualities, our spiritual gifts, in the power of the Holy Spirit, the world will be rocked on its heels by the force of our love and our witness. The proof that God is real and active in the world is the proof that we demonstrate in our lives.

We demonstrate God's reality and power when we have learned the secret set forth in the next chapter, the famous Love Chapter of the New Testament, 1 Corinthians 13. The most startling aspect of Paul's description of love—considering how the word love has come to be defined in our

> **The body of Christ functions by the exercise of its gifts, and every Christian has at least one gift.**

The Love Chapter

culture as a warm-fuzzy feeling or even as sex—is the way he defines love not as an emotion but as a decision and as an act of the will:

Love is patient, love is kind. It does not envy, it does not boast, it is not proud. It is not rude, it is not self-seeking, it is not easily angered, it keeps no record of wrongs. Love does not delight in evil but rejoices with the truth. It always protects, always trusts, always hopes, always perseveres. Love never fails (vv. 4–8).

The Gift of Tongues — In chapter 14, Paul takes up another problem that was causing confusion in the church: the misuse of one of the gifts—the gift of tongues. The false use of tongues is a problem in our society today as it was when Paul addressed it in this chapter. To correct these abuses, Paul attempts to focus this section on the importance of the gift of prophecy. It is always amazing to me how many read this chapter and entirely miss the apostle's point. The whole purpose of the chapter is to encourage those with the gift of prophecy to exercise it. But you hardly ever hear anything about that today. These days, we hear a lot about tongues but very little about prophecy. Yet Paul was trying to play down the gift of tongues and play up the gift of prophecy, which is the ability to explain and expound the Scriptures, to speak comfort and edification and encouragement from the Scriptures.

The Resurrection — Chapter 15 places great emphasis on the Resurrection, and for good reason. What would any of these truths be worth if we did not have a living Christ to make them real? The Resurrection is the great pivot upon which the entire Christian faith balances. Without the Resurrection, all else that is Christianity collapses. If Jesus Christ was not raised from the dead, then, as the apostle says in this chapter, we are hopeless, and not only that, we are the most to be pitied of all people—we are nuts, we are fools, we ought to be locked up somewhere.

> **The Resurrection is the great pivot upon which the entire Christian faith balances.**

But praise God, the Resurrection was a real event. It did not occur in someone's imagination; it occurred in history, in time and space.

Jesus is alive! And that is why Paul can close chapter 15 with this word of confidence and encouragement:

My dear brothers, stand firm. Let nothing move you. Always give yourselves fully to the work of the Lord, because you know that your labor in the Lord is not in vain (v. 58).

Chapter 16 is Paul's postscript in which he catches up on certain matters that the church needed to know about, such as the need to take a regular collection, the commending of certain missionaries, Paul's personal plans, and a few last-moment words of encouragement:

> *Be on your guard; stand firm in the faith; be men of courage; be strong. Do everything in love (vv. 13–14).*

Like the first-century Corinthians, we live in a world of pressures, temptations, and constant spiritual and moral battles. But you and I have everything we need to win the victory. We have the spiritualities of God, and these are more than enough to make us super-conquerors over the carnalities of the flesh and Satan.

NOTES

NOTES

CHAPTER FOUR

2 CORINTHIANS: WHEN I AM WEAK, I AM STRONG

SOME YEARS AGO, I VISITED THE CITY OF CORINTH. There is little left standing of the original city, which was destroyed by the Romans a few years after Paul's visit there and has been in ruins ever since. Some temple columns remain, however, as well as the marketplace and other public areas of the city, and the actual pavement of the judgment hall of the Roman pro-consul is well preserved.

In Paul's day, Corinth was a center of pleasure, a center of public discourse and philosophical debate, and a great commercial city. It was a city of great beauty, with many richly adorned temples to pagan gods and goddesses. As we said in the previous chapter, Corinth also was the center of lascivious worship—the worship of the goddess of love, Aphrodite. Her temple was the site where some ten thousand temple prostitutes (for that's exactly what a priestess of Aphrodite was) carried on their trade. Corinth was a sex-saturated society, and you can see indications of this in Paul's letters to the Corinthian church.

As I stood among the ruins of the city of Priscilla and Aquila, where Paul had preached and labored for God while supporting himself as a tentmaker, I couldn't help thinking of certain phrases that come right out of Paul's second letter to the church at Corinth, one of the most personal and emotional of all his letters.

The Background of Second Corinthians

To understand this letter, it's important to grasp the background and context in which it was written. After Paul had established the church in Corinth and labored in the city for almost two years, he moved on to the city of Ephesus on the Asian mainland. From there he wrote his first letter to the Corinthians in order to correct some of the divisions that had arisen in the church at Corinth as well as to deal with some of the scandals that had rocked the church. After Paul had written that first letter, a group of people who wanted to reintroduce hard-line, legalistic Judaism into Christianity caused a great deal of trouble in the church and gained a great deal of influence over the people. This group was headed by a teacher who opposed Paul and had probably come over from Jerusalem, infecting the church and teaching the people that they had to observe the Law of Moses. Calling themselves the "Christ party," they represented themselves as the only true followers of Christ and the law of God, and they claimed that the great themes of grace taught by Paul were not authentic Christianity. Paul makes reference to these people who claim to follow only Christ in his first letter (see 1 Cor. 1:12).

This faction apparently took over the church in Corinth, so Paul revisited the city for a short time and apparently was rebuffed by the church leaders. The very church Paul had planted had become so permeated with false Christianity that Paul himself was not welcome there!

Paul returned to Ephesus, and from there he wrote a short, sharp, emotional letter, rebuking and reproving the Corinthian Christians for allowing themselves to be misled. That particular letter has been lost to us, but it is clear that Paul penned such a letter (see 2 Cor. 2:3–4). We do not know why it was not preserved—perhaps because Paul, writing in anger, said things that went beyond what the Holy Spirit intended. Or perhaps that letter simply dealt with temporal matters of the Corinthian church—matters that would not be meaningful to us today. In any case, that lost letter certainly did not have the force of Scripture. If God had wanted that letter saved, it would not have been lost.

> The very church Paul had planted had become so permeated with false Christianity that Paul himself was not welcome there!

That letter was carried to the church at Corinth by Titus, while the apostle remained in Ephesus, anxiously waiting to hear what the Corinthians' response would be. This is what Paul is referring to in the opening of 2 Corinthians when he tells them that he has been anxious and concerned about them.

> *I wrote you out of great distress and anguish of heart and with many tears, not to grieve you but to let you know the depth of my love for you (2:4).*

He also tells them that he has undergone intense suffering while waiting in Ephesus for word from them.

> *We do not want you to be uninformed, brothers, about the hardships we suffered in the province of Asia. We were under great pressure, far beyond our ability to endure, so that we despaired even of life. Indeed, in our hearts we felt the sentence of death. But this happened that we might not rely on ourselves but on God, who raises the dead (1:8–9).*

While Paul was waiting for a response from the Corinthian church, trouble arose in the church at Ephesus. This trouble is recorded in Acts 19. There, the silversmiths caused a great commotion in the city, and Paul was threatened with being dragged before the Roman judges. He escaped and decided to go on to Macedonia to meet Titus, who would be coming up through Macedonia on his return from Corinth; and because his anxiety over the Corinthians was so great, he could wait no longer for news. He also intended to raise money there for the relief of the Christians in Jerusalem, who were suffering from a famine.

With these two concerns weighing heavily on his heart, Paul went to Philippi in Macedonia. There he met Titus and received word that the sharp letter he had written to the Corinthians had accomplished its work. The majority of the Corinthian Christians had repented of their rejection of his ministry and had begun to live again the life of Jesus Christ.

A minority was still unyielding, however, and continued to rebel against the authority of the apostle. So, from the city of Philippi, Paul wrote this letter, 2 Corinthians, which expresses so much of the anxiety and agitation of heart that he experienced.

The Outline of Second Corinthians

Out of his tears and heartache, and the passion with which Paul writes, come the great spiritual themes embodied in this letter. Here, then is a structural overview of Paul's second letter to the church at Corinth:

Ministry within the Church (2 Corinthians 1–4)

1.	Introduction	1:1–11
2.	Paul's change of plans, inability to come to Corinth	1:12–2:4
3.	Forgive and restore the repentant sinner	2:5–13
4.	Christ causes us to triumph	2:14–17
5.	Paul's ministry: a ministry of changed lives, a ministry of the new covenant, a ministry of Christ	3:1–4:7
6.	The trials of ministry	4:8–15
7.	Our motivation for serving God	4:16–18

Giving and Service by the Church (2 Corinthians 5–10)

8.	Our future reward for serving Christs	5:1–16
9.	The ministry of reconciliation	5:17–21
10.	Giving no offense to others	6:1–10

**Authority and Wise Exercise of Church Leadership
(2 Corinthians 11–13)**

Ministry within the Church

In the opening chapters of the second letter to the Corinthians we discover a declaration of what true Christian ministry ought to be. As Paul states in chapter 3, for instance, it is not the ministry of the old covenant but of the new. In other words, the message is not the demand of the law upon people to compel them to follow certain rules and regulations. When Christianity becomes a set of do's and don'ts, it always becomes a deadly, stultifying, dangerous thing. At that point, it is no longer a living relationship with a loving Lord but a grim determination to cross all the t's and dot all the i's of the law. These are demands made upon the flesh. As Paul says, the old covenant, exemplified by the Ten Commandments, makes its demands upon us but without an accompanying dynamic to fulfill it. It is a ministry of death. As he writes in 2 Corinthians 3:6:

> *He has made us competent as ministers of a new covenant—not of the letter but of the Spirit; for the letter kills, but the Spirit gives life.*

Next, Paul traces the history of the new covenant—the new arrangement for living. This is not the old grim determination to clench your

The New
Covenant

fists and set your teeth and try to do what God demands—that is not true Christianity. The new covenant relationship is the realization that He has provided the Holy Spirit to minister the life of a risen Lord in your life. The same power that raised Him from the dead is available to you as strength and grace to do all that life demands of you. That is the new arrangement for living. And here we find the exciting resources of the Christian life.

> **The same power that raised Him from the dead is available to you as strength and grace to do all that life demands of you.**

First resource: the Word of God. The business of a minister of Jesus Christ (and remember, all Christians are called to be His ministers—not just pastors and teachers) is to declare the Word of God. Notice how Paul puts it:

> *Since through God's mercy we have this ministry, we do not lose heart. Rather, we have renounced secret and shameful ways; we do not use deception, nor do we distort the word of God. On the contrary, by setting forth the truth plainly we commend ourselves to every man's conscience in the sight of God (4:1–2).*

Here we see not only the failure of the first-century church, but of today's church in so many areas—clever, subtle tampering with the Word of God, undermining its authority, subverting its message, ignoring its witness, refusing to act upon its truth.

Second resource: the mysterious indwelling treasure of the Spirit of God. Paul addresses this resource in 2 Corinthians 4:7:

> *We have this treasure in jars of clay to show that this all-surpassing power is from God and not from us.*

> **The power of a victorious life comes from the Spirit of God, not from us.**

Victorious living does not come from a charming personality or by being clever or educated. Victorious Christian living comes from this treasure hidden inside the earthen vessel of our lives. The power of a victorious life comes from the Spirit of God, not from us. This is the secret by which God's power is released in our lives.

Third resource: hope. Paul goes on to declare the great hope of the believer:

*We fix our eyes not on what is seen, but on what is unseen. For
what is seen is temporary, but what is unseen is eternal (4:18).*

We have a body that cannot be destroyed—"an eternal house in heaven,"
as 5:1 tells us, "not built by human hands." God has a great future ahead
for us. The life we now live is the preparation for that life that is to come.
The present is but a prologue to the future.

Chapter 5 also reveals the radical transformation that takes place when
we commit ourselves to Christ. In verse 17, Paul writes:

*If anyone is in Christ, he is a new creation; the old has gone, the
new has come!*

We are new in Christ, and, as a result, God has given us a new ministry
and a new message: the ministry and message of reconciliation:

*All this is from God, who reconciled us to himself through Christ
and gave us the ministry of reconciliation: that God was reconciling
the world to himself in Christ, not counting men's sins against them.
And he has committed to us the message of reconciliation (5:18–19).*

That is our theme. That is our banner headline, unfurled before all the
people of the earth: You can be reconciled to God through faith in Jesus
Christ. With that as our message and ministry, we have become what Paul
calls ambassadors for Christ, His representatives to the world:

*We are therefore Christ's ambassadors, as though God were making
his appeal through us. We implore you on Christ's behalf: Be reconciled to God. God made him who had no sin to be sin for us, so
that in him we might become the righteousness of God (5:20–21).*

That is the gospel in a nutshell.

Giving and Service by the Church

In chapters 8 and 9 we find Paul's declaration of the giving and service
ministry of the church. Because of the great famine in Jerusalem, Paul
was taking up a collection for the physical relief of the saints in that city.
Giving, says Paul, is the proof of genuine Christian love, and he appeals

to the Corinthian believers to open their hearts to give, just as they have received from Jesus Christ:

> *For you know the grace of our Lord Jesus Christ, that though he was rich, yet for your sakes he became poor, so that you through his poverty might become rich (8:9).*

Here, as in many places in Scripture, we see a spiritual paradox at work: Christianity operates in poverty, making many rich. Jesus, the Creator of the universe, set aside His riches and entered into His creation in a state of poverty in order to enrich us all by His grace. He is our pattern. We are to give in order to enrich others with the grace of Jesus Christ.

This passage is not a justification for high-pressure financial campaigns or efforts to shame Christians into giving. Under God's economy, nobody is to be put under any compulsion. We are to give according to personal conscience. As Paul writes:

> *Remember this: Whoever sows sparingly will also reap sparingly, and whoever sows generously will also reap generously. Each man should give what he has decided in his heart to give, not reluctantly or under compulsion, for God loves a cheerful giver. And God is able to make all grace abound to you, so that in all things at all times, having all that you need, you will abound in every good work (9:6–8).*

Have you dared to put God's economic plan to the test? His Word is as true in our century as it was in the first century.

Authority and Wise Exercise of Church Leadership

In chapters 10, 11, and 12, Paul's tone changes as he begins to address the rebellious minority of Christians in Corinth who were still refusing the authority of his ministry among them. He wasn't confronting their disobedience to him, but to the truth of God. These false teachers had exalted themselves on the basis of their lineage, their background, and their education. They were prideful and arrogant, and the apostle Paul takes on the entire basis of their arrogant claim to be leaders of the people.

In an ironic, almost sarcastic fashion, Paul shows these pretentious leaders the true basis of authority, and he does so by contrasting the credentials they care so much about (status, background, and education) with the credentials God gives (the knowledge of God). Paul is saying, in effect, "If you insist upon being impressed by these worldly symbols of authority, well I could boast before you too. If I did, I would be a fool. But since you are so impressed by such things, very well, I'll play your foolish game and boast a little. I'll tell you what God has done through me."

And then there comes this great passage:

> *What anyone else dares to boast about—I am speaking as a fool— I also dare to boast about. Are they Hebrews? So am I. Are they Israelites? So am I. Are they Abraham's descendants? So am I. Are they servants of Christ? (I am out of my mind to talk like this.) I am more. I have worked much harder, been in prison more frequently, been flogged more severely, and been exposed to death again and again. Five times I received from the Jews the forty lashes minus one. Three times I was beaten with rods, once I was stoned, three times I was shipwrecked, I spent a night and a day in the open sea, I have been constantly on the move. I have been in danger from rivers, in danger from bandits, in danger from my own countrymen, in danger from Gentiles; in danger in the city, in danger in the country, in danger at sea; and in danger from false brothers. I have labored and toiled and have often gone without sleep; I have known hunger and thirst and have often gone without food; I have been cold and naked. Besides everything else, I face daily the pressure of my concern for all the churches. Who is weak, and I do not feel weak? Who is led into sin, and I do not inwardly burn?*
>
> *If I must boast, I will boast of the things that show my weakness (11:21–30).*

Incredible credentials! Yet these, Paul is quick to add, are mere foolishness, idle boasts. "This is not where my authority lies," he is saying. "If you really want to know where my authority lies and where true spiritual power comes from, let me tell you how I began to learn the lesson. This is not going to sound very impressive, but I want you to know that I am telling you the truth. This is the event I boast about more than anything else in my life—the moment when I began to learn the secret of genuine power."

And, beginning with 11:31, Paul describes the time he had to be let down over the city wall of Damascus, just so that he could slink away into the darkness from the pursuing guards of King Aretas—as if he were a common thief! This is not a story of great victory and valor; it's a story of defeat and discouragement. Yet this is the story, Paul says, of the day he learned the secret of effective, victorious Christian living: "When I am weak, then I am strong."

> **Paul learned the secret of effective, victorious Christian living: "When I am weak, then I am strong."**

He goes on in 12:6–10 to describe his thorn in the flesh—some ugly, painful aspect of his life, perhaps some physical affliction—and how he prayed earnestly three times that God would remove it. But God knew best, and God allowed Paul to keep his thorn in the flesh. God's message to Paul was:

> *"My grace is sufficient for you, for my power is made perfect in weakness." Therefore I will boast all the more gladly about my weaknesses, so that Christ's power may rest on me. That is why, for Christ's sake, I delight in weaknesses, in insults, in hardships, in persecutions, in difficulties. For when I am weak, then I am strong (12:9–10).*

That is the secret of true Christian strength. Not outward impressiveness. Not great prestige, pomp, and favor. Not degrees and honors and awards. No. Spiritual power never lies in the place of human pride and might. Neither does it lie in a brilliant, impressive personality nor in ability to speak with eloquent oratory. Spiritual power is found in the heart of the humble human being who fully recognizes his or her dependence on the living Lord within. The weaker you are, the stronger Christ can be.

> **Spiritual power is found in the heart of the humble human being who fully recognizes his or her dependence on the living Lord within.**

In an epistle rich with meaning, this is perhaps the richest truth of all: Out of weakness comes strength.

So Paul closes the epistle by addressing the people at Corinth as he addresses us today,

> *Examine yourselves to see whether you are in the faith; test yourselves (13:5).*

Do you truly believe and trust God, even in your times of trial and weakness? Are you counting on His strength rather than your own? Are you walking boldly into situations and going out on limbs for Him—not foolishly, but trustingly, knowing that He has led you there and wants to use you in your weakness, so that His might and power might be demonstrated to a watching world? That is the great secret of true Christian living:

Our weakness—His strength!

NOTES

NOTES

ADVENTURING
through
PAUL'S EPISTLES

CHAPTER FIVE

GALATIANS:
HOW *to* BE FREE

TWO OF THE GREAT LEADERS of the American Revolution in 1776 were the American-born Benjamin Franklin and the Englishman Thomas Paine. Once, as these two men were discussing their passionate belief in the concept of liberty, Franklin commented, "Wherever liberty is, there is my country."

Paine replied, "Wherever liberty is *not*, there is my country." In other words, Paine was committed to going wherever there was oppression and injustice and seeking to bring liberty to those countries. And he did so, passionately working for liberty—at great personal cost—in England, America, and France.

Paine's attitude is much like that of the apostle Paul, as expressed in his great epistle to the Galatians. Seeing both political and religious oppression on every hand, seeing people bound up and held down by laws and rules and legalism, the apostle Paul saw a large part of his mission as one of going wherever liberty was *not*, in order to bring freedom to people whose spirits and souls were in chains.

Our Spiritual "Emancipation Proclamation"

Galatians is probably the most colorful epistle in the New Testament, filled with vivid, forceful language. It is closely related to the epistles to the Romans and Hebrews. These three New Testament letters—Romans, Galatians, and Hebrews—form what might be regarded as an inspired commentary on a single verse from the Old Testament book of Habakkuk:

> *The righteous will live by his faith (2:4).*

All three of these New Testament letters quote this verse, and each of them offers a different aspect or dimension of it.

In Romans, Paul places the emphasis on the words "the righteous," detailing what it means to be righteous and how a person becomes justified before God and declared righteous in Christ. It was the epistle to the Romans that delivered Martin Luther from his terrible legalism and showed him the truth of God's grace through faith.

In Hebrews, the emphasis is on the last words "by . . . faith." This is the great New Testament treatise on faith, culminating in that memorable section on the heroes of the faith in Hebrews 11, demonstrating that salvation by faith has always been by grace through faith, both in the Old Testament and in the New.

> Galatians is probably the most colorful epistle in the New Testament.

In Galatians, Paul places the emphasis upon the words "shall live" as he comes to grips with the question of what real Christian life is like. The answer can be framed in a single word: liberty. This is the letter of Christian liberty, the fullest expression of life and faith. As Christians, we are called to liberty in Jesus Christ, and the goal of this epistle is that Christians might discover the liberty of the children of God in accordance with all that God has planned for humanity in the way of freedom and enjoyment. Paul wants us to experience freedom to the utmost in our spirits, restrained only as necessary to be in harmony with the design of God. So it is with good reason that this letter has been called the Bill of Rights of the Christian Life, or the Magna Carta of Christian Liberty, or Our Spiritual Emancipation Proclamation—emancipation from all forms of legalism and bondage in the Christian experience.

> Galatians is the letter of Christian liberty.

The Outline of Galatians

Here is an overview of the structure of Paul's epistle to the Galatians:

The Gospel of Liberty—Justification (Galatians 1–4)

1. Introduction: Why have the Galatians departed from this gospel of liberty? — 1:1–9
2. The gospel of liberty came directly from God — 1:10–24
3. The gospel of liberty affirmed in Jerusalem and by Paul's rebuke to Peter — 2
4. Salvation comes by faith, not works or the Law — 3–4

How to Live Freely—Sanctification (Galatians 5–6)

5. Stand fast in your liberty — 5:1–12
6. In liberty, love one another — 5:13–15
7. Walk in the Spirit, not the flesh — 5:16–21
8. The fruit of the Spirit — 5:22–26
9. Live free, do good to all, care for one another — 6:1–10
10. Conclusion, including a curse upon those who impose their legalism on believers under grace — 6:11–18

The Unique Identity of the Galatians

Unlike the letters written to a single church, as in the cases of the letters to Corinth and Ephesus, this letter is addressed to a number of churches. In the introduction of the letter we read:

> *Paul, an apostle—sent not from men nor by man, but by Jesus Christ and God the Father, who raised him from the dead—and all the brothers with me,*
>   *To the churches in Galatia (1:1–2).*

The Galatian churches, described in Acts 13 and 14, were established by Paul on his first missionary journey, when he traveled with Barnabas into the cities of Antioch, Iconium, Derbe, and Lystra. In Lystra, he was first welcomed and honored as a god, then later stoned and dragged outside the city and left for dead. In fact, he experienced persecution in every one of the cities in the region of Galatia.

The name of the province comes from the same root as the word *Gaul,* the ancient Roman name for parts of Western Europe, including what is now France. About three hundred years before Christ, Gauls had invaded the Roman Empire and sacked the city of Rome. Then they crossed into northern Greece and continued across the Dardanelles straits into Asia Minor (modern Turkey). At the invitation of one of the kings of the area, they settled there.

So the Galatians were not Arabs or Turks or Asians. They were a Celtic race, of ancestry similar to that of the Scots, the Irish, the Britons, and the French. Julius Caesar described the Gauls as "fickle in their resolves, fond of change and not to be trusted." Or, as another ancient writer put it, "They are frank, impetuous, impressionable, eminently intelligent, fond of show but extremely inconstant, the fruit of excessive vanity."

On his second missionary journey, accompanied this time by Silas, Paul again visited these Galatian cities and the churches that had been established there. On this second journey, he spent a considerable time in various cities of the region because he became sick. He refers to this illness in a rather oblique manner in this letter. Evidently it was some kind of serious eye trouble, for he says to the Galatians:

> *Even though my illness was a trial to you, you did not treat me with contempt or scorn. Instead, you welcomed me as if I were an angel of God, as if I were Christ Jesus himself. . . . I can testify*

*that, if you could have done so, you would have torn out your eyes
and given them to me (4:14–15).*

Some Bible scholars feel he had inflamed eyes that made him seem repulsive. Yet, these Galatians received him with great joy, treating him as though he were an angel of God or even Christ Jesus Himself. They reveled in the gospel of grace he brought because he had disclosed to them—with brilliant, vivid clarity—the glory and the work of the crucified Lord. As a result, they had entered into the fullness of life by the Spirit and had received the love, joy, and peace that Jesus Christ gives when He enters the human heart.

The Apostle's Anger

But as Paul writes this letter to the Christians in the region of Galatia (he is probably writing from the city of Corinth), it is evident that something has happened. Certain people, whom Paul labels in another place "wolves" (see Acts 20:29), had come among them. Who were these wolves? They were Judaizers—hardened legalists who had come down from Jerusalem with what Paul calls "an alien gospel," a mixture of Christianity and the practices of Judaism. The gospel of the Judaizers was not a totally different gospel, but a perversion of the true gospel. To these Gentile believers, who had just received from Paul the fresh, liberating gospel of Jesus Christ, these wolves declared a gospel of bondage, a gospel of laws, rules, and rituals. In order to become genuine Christians, they claimed, the Gentiles would have to become circumcised, keep the Law of Moses, and obey all the Old Testament regulations. These legalists were trying to impose all the restrictions and the ceremonial obligations of the Law of Moses.

> To these Gentile believers, who had just received from Paul the fresh, liberating gospel of Jesus Christ, these wolves declared a gospel of bondage, a gospel of laws, rules, and rituals.

What about Jesus Christ and His complete work upon the cross? Well, these Judaizers hadn't set Jesus Christ aside totally. Like most false gospels, the false gospel of the Judaizers maintained an outer shell of Christianity. But the heart of this false gospel was not grace and faith; it was works. The Lord Jesus Christ was given a secondary place in this gospel. Keeping the rules and rituals of the old Law of Moses was paramount.

Moreover, the Judaizers challenged the apostolic authority of Paul. They challenged him for being (in their view) independent, undependable, and overly enthusiastic. They even claimed he had graduated from the wrong seminary! They were trying to get the Galatians to reject his authority as an apostle.

Paul was greatly disturbed by this news, and his agitation and anger come through loud and clear! Listen to some of the expressions he uses:

> *Even if we or an angel from heaven should preach a gospel other than the one we preached to you, let him be eternally condemned! (1:8).*

To put it bluntly, Paul is saying that anyone who preaches a different gospel than the one he has already preached should be damned to hell! That should leave no doubt about the strength of the apostle's feelings on this matter. He repeats the same sentiments in the very next verse:

> *As we have already said, so now I say again: If anybody is preaching to you a gospel other than what you accepted, let him be eternally condemned! (1:9).*

> **Those who reject His grace and seek to work their own way to God through rituals or their own righteousness are accursed, as the full range of the New Testament makes clear.**

When we hear such words as *damned,* we think of curses and insults. But Paul is not being profane or indecent. He is simply facing the fact that any who come with a different gospel have already damned themselves. Such people have rejected the truth of the grace of Jesus Christ. Those who reject His grace and seek to work their own way to God through rituals or their own righteousness are accursed, as the full range of the New Testament makes clear.

At the close of the letter, Paul's emotions are stirred against those who preach circumcision and legalism instead of the liberating grace of Jesus:

> *As for those agitators, I wish they would go the whole way and emasculate themselves! (5:12).*

In other words, "Since the Judaizers are so zealous to put Christians under bondage to circumcision, I wish that, while they're at it, they would completely remove their manhood!"

Here you clearly see the fire that flashes throughout this letter. The apostle is deeply disturbed. In fact, Paul is so intense and passionate that he can't even wait for a secretary to take dictation. Despite his poor eyesight, he painfully, indignantly scrawls this epistle out in his own large-lettered hand.

Why is the apostle so angry with these Judaizers? Because they have perverted the purity of the gospel. And in doing so, they have attempted to re-enslave those who are just becoming free through the grace of Jesus Christ. They are undoing everything Paul himself is trying to accomplish by preaching the gospel of salvation by grace through faith in Jesus Christ.

The gospel is simplicity itself: first, Christ gave Himself for our sins—that's *justification*; second, Christ gave Himself to deliver us from this present evil age—that's *sanctification*. All of it is by grace and not by works. It is the assault upon these truths that has so deeply disturbed the apostle. He knows that injecting legalism into Christianity kills the very heartbeat of the gospel and leads people back into bondage, failure, and misery.

These two aspects of the gospel—justification and sanctification—make up the basic outline of the letter to the Galatians.

The Gospel of Liberty

Chapters 1 through 4 of this epistle deal with justification by faith. Christ died for our sins—that's the basic declaration of the gospel, the good news that Christ has borne our sins. So Paul spends Galatians 1 defending this good news.

First he shows that it was revealed by Jesus Christ directly to him. He didn't get it from anyone, not even from the apostles. Christ Himself appeared to Paul and told him this good news. Paul writes,

> *I want you to know, brothers, that the gospel I preached is not something that man made up. I did not receive it from any man, nor was I taught it; rather, I received it by revelation from Jesus Christ (1:11–12).*

Second, this was acknowledged by the other apostles as being the same gospel they received. Some people have claimed that Paul preached a different gospel than Peter, James, John, and the others—that Paul's gospel is superior to theirs. But Paul himself in this letter says that fourteen years after his conversion, he went up to Jerusalem and had an opportunity to compare notes with the other apostles. When he did so, the other apostles were amazed to discover that this man, who had never been a part of the original twelve, knew as much about the truth of the gospel as they did. In fact, he knew what had gone on in the secret, intimate gatherings that they had had with the Lord Jesus Christ. You can see an example of this in 1 Corinthians, where the apostle describes the Lord's Supper. He says:

> *I received from the Lord what I also passed on to you: The Lord Jesus, on the night he was betrayed, took bread, and when he had given thanks, he broke it and said, "This is my body, which is for you; do this in remembrance of me" (1 Cor. 11:23–24).*

How did Paul know all of this? He received it directly from the Lord Jesus. So when Peter, James, and John heard that this man knew as much about what had gone on in that Upper Room as they did, they recognized that here indeed was a man called of God. His apostleship, which came directly from Jesus Christ, rested upon that fact.

Third, it was not only revealed to him by Christ and acknowledged by the other apostles, but it was vindicated when Peter came to Antioch.

Peter, the ostensible leader of the apostles, was in error in Antioch. You can read the story in Galatians 2:11–21. The difficulty between Peter and Paul was the matter of eating kosher foods versus Gentile foods. Peter was a Jew, raised to eat nothing but kosher foods; but when he became a follower of Christ, he ate with the Gentiles and thus indicated the liberty he had in Christ. But when certain men came down from Jerusalem, he began to compromise and went back to eating only with Jews, thus denying the very liberty that he had formerly proclaimed. This is what stirred up Paul and made him angry with Peter—publicly and to his face. Think of that! This maverick apostle challenged Peter the Rock! And he vindicated the gospel as he did so.

Salvation by Faith, Not Works

In chapters 2 through 4, Paul shows us that the gospel is about salvation by faith and not by works. Jesus has done everything to secure our salvation; we can do nothing to secure our salvation. Moreover, our salvation is the result of a promise and not the law. This promise predates the Law of Moses, having been given to Abraham four hundred years before Moses was born. The Law, therefore, cannot change the promise. The promise of God stands true whether the Law comes in or not.

Paul also shows that those who are in Christ are children, not slaves.

They are no longer servants; they are part of the family of God. In this connection, he deals with the great allegorical passages concerning Hagar and Sarah, the law, and the mountain of grace (Jerusalem that is above; see Gal. 4:25–26). From these passages he declares the great fact of justification by faith.

This was the truth that delivered the soul of Martin Luther, the monk of Wittenberg who nailed his Ninety-Five Theses to the door of the castle church and thereby began what we call the Protestant Reformation. Here was a man who had tried to find his way to heaven on the pathway of works. He had done everything the church of his day demanded. He had tried fasting, indulgences, the sacraments, the intercession of the saints, penances, and confessions. He had endured nightlong vigils and heavy days of labor. But the harder he worked, the more his inner distress increased. Justification by Faith

Finally, in desperation, he went to the head of his Augustinian order and asked for some kind of release. The dear old man who headed the order knew little about the Word of God, so miserable was the condition of the organized church at that time. Yet he did tell Luther one thing: "Put your faith not in yourself but in the wounds of Christ."

A dim ray of light broke through to Martin Luther's soul. But it wasn't until he was in his little room in the tower, preparing lectures on the Psalms for his students, that the full light of awareness suddenly shone upon him. He was struck by a verse in the Psalms:

> In you, O LORD, I have taken refuge; let me never be put to shame; deliver me in your righteousness (Ps. 31:1).

This verse gripped Martin Luther's heart as he suddenly realized that the righteousness of God was to him a terrible thing. He saw it as an unbending righteous judgment by which God would destroy everyone who failed in the least degree to measure up to the full expectation of the holiness of God. Luther said that he even hated the word *righteousness*.

But then, as he began to investigate the Word, it led him to the epistle to the Romans where he read these words: "The righteous shall live by faith." That struck fire in his heart, and he saw for the first time that Another had already paid the penalty for sin so that he himself didn't have to. Christ had entered the human race and carried our guilt so that God might, in justice, accept us—not according to our merits or righteousness, but according to His.

Martin Luther was never the same man again. This discovery led him to challenge the system of indulgences and all the other legalistic practices that kept people in bondage to the organized church and moved him to nail the theses to the door.

The Unique Gospel

> Every religion known to humanity is a religion of works—except the gospel of Jesus Christ!

It is interesting, as someone has pointed out, that every single religion known to humanity is a religion of works—*except the gospel of Jesus Christ!* Hinduism tells us that if we renounce the world and relate ourselves to the "spirit of the universe," we will at last find our way to peace. Buddhism sets before us eight principles by which human beings are to walk and thus find themselves on the way to salvation. Judaism says we must keep the Law absolutely and inflexibly and then we will be saved. Islam says that a person must pray five times a day and give alms and fast during the month of Ramadan and obey the commands of Allah. Unitarianism says that people are saved by having good character. Modern humanism says salvation is achieved through service to humankind. In every one of these religions, salvation is said to be attained by something we must do.

But the good news of the gospel is that Jesus Christ has done it all! He *alone* has done what no one can do for himself or herself. *And He has set us free.*

How to Live Freely

In Galatians 5 and 6, Paul turns to the second and equally important aspect of the gospel, summarized in these words:

> *[The Lord Jesus Christ] gave himself for our sins* to rescue us from the present evil age, *according to the will of our God and Father (1:4).*

Christianity is not solely about going to heaven when you die (justification). It is also about living now in this present life (sanctification). It is being set free from bondage to the world and its ways, its evil and wickedness. It is being liberated in the here and now. This, too, is by the gift of Jesus Christ. He came not only to deliver us from death, but also from this present evil age. How does He deliver us in the here and now? By living His life through us. That is the key to sanctification.

We know that this age is evil. We feel its pressures to conform, to lower our standards, to believe all the lies shouted at us by TV, films, popular music, and the people around us. But we fall into the trap of thinking that we can deliver ourselves! So we set up our Christian programs, we fill our days with activity, we teach Sunday school, we sing in the choir, we join a Bible study or a Christian group—and we think that we are free. These are all good things, of course, but they do not save us. If we think we are saved by all the good religious things we do, we are still in bondage. We are sunk to our eyeballs in Galatianism. We have fallen into the same bondage that had crept into the Galatian churches. We are living by works—not by faith.

The Key to Sanctification

In the closing two chapters of Galatians, we see that the whole point of our Christian walk is to repudiate the life of the flesh with its self-centeredness and to rely upon the work of the Spirit of God to reproduce in us the life of Jesus Christ. This is all gathered up for us in one of the best-known verses of the entire letter:

> *I have been crucified with Christ and I no longer live, but Christ lives in me. The life I live in the body, I live by faith in the Son of God, who loved me and gave himself for me (2:20).*

The old self-centered "I" has been crucified with Christ so that it no longer has any right to live. Your task and mine is to see that it doesn't live, that it is repudiated, that it is put aside, along with its determination to express what Paul calls "the works of the flesh"—such acts as those listed in 5:19–21: sexual immorality, impurity, and debauchery; idolatry and witchcraft (a word that, in the original Greek, is linked to abuse of drugs for mind-altering, mood-altering purposes); hatred, discord, jealousy, fits of rage, selfish ambition, dissensions, factions, and envy; drunkenness, orgies, and the like. All of these ugly acts are the works of the flesh—the old self-centered life that, Paul declares, was judged and cut off at the cross, to be replaced by the life of Jesus Christ shining through us.

Instead of being controlled by the flesh, our lives are to show a growing evidence of control by the Spirit of God. The evidence that God is gradually sanctifying us and taking control of more and more of our lives is found in Galatians 5:22–23, in a list of character qualities that Paul calls "the fruit of the Spirit"—love, joy, peace, patience, kindness, goodness, faithfulness, gentleness, and self-control.

> Instead of being controlled by the flesh, our lives are to show a growing evidence of control by the Spirit of God.

Now this is where Christian liberty enters in. You haven't begun to live as God intended you to live until the fruit of the Spirit is a consistent manifestation in your life. Anything less is the bondage of legalism, with its frustration, fear, and failure.

In Galatians 6, Paul describes how being filled with the Spirit enables us to experience true fellowship with each other in the body of Christ. When our lives show evidence of the indwelling of God's Spirit, we begin doing the things that lead to wholeness, health, and unity in the body of Christ. We begin bearing one another's burdens, restoring one another in meekness and gentleness. We begin giving generously and freely to meet one another's needs, and we begin sowing to the Spirit instead of to the flesh.

> When our lives show evidence of the indwelling of God's Spirit, we begin doing the things that lead to wholeness, health, and unity in the body of Christ.

Paul's Personal P.S.

Paul closes his letter to the Galatians with one of the most intensely personal postscripts in the entire New Testament. He writes,

See what large letters I use as I write to you with my own hand! (6:11).

Painfully scrawling each letter, hampered by poor eyesight, he says in effect, "I do not glory in my flesh like these Judaizers do. They love to compel people to be circumcised, because to them each person circumcised is another scalp they can hang on their belts as a sign they have done something tremendous for God. That is not my glory. I glory only in the cross of Christ—and the cross cuts off that kind of living. The cross destroys the 'old man' with all his arrogance, ambition, and self-glorification."

Paul knows that his strong words in this powerful epistle will stir up anger and even opposition among some in the church, but he is ready for it. He writes:

Let no one cause me trouble, for I bear on my body the marks of Jesus (6:17).

In other words, "If anyone wants to oppose me or make life hard for me—don't even think it! I want you to know that living this kind of life has been costly for me. I have earned the hatred and persecution of many.

I bear in my body the scars of serving the Lord Jesus."

If you challenge the world and its ways—and even if you challenge worldliness in the church—you will be resented, even hated. You will be shining the light of God's truth upon them, and they resent it. But you need to courageously follow the example of the apostle Paul when he says, in effect, "It doesn't make any difference to me. I am scarred and battered and beaten, but I glory in the Lord Jesus Christ who has taught me what true liberty is. Wherever liberty is not, wherever people are being held in bondage and ignorance and oppression, wherever the grace of Jesus Christ is being subordinated to rituals and rules, that is where I will go. In the name of Jesus Christ, I will go where He sends me and say what He tells me to say, and I will point the way to liberty."

NOTES

NOTES

CHAPTER SIX

EPHESIANS:
THE CALLING
of the SAINTS

THE EPISTLE TO THE EPHESIANS is, in many ways, the crowning glory of the New Testament. It would probably surprise you, however, to learn that this letter probably shouldn't be called "Ephesians." The fact is, we don't really know to whom it was written. The Christians at Ephesus were certainly among the recipients of this letter, but undoubtedly there were others. In many of the original Greek manuscripts there is actually a blank where the King James Version and the New International Version insert the words "at Ephesus." That is why the Revised Standard Version does not say, "To the saints at Ephesus," but simply, "To the saints who are also faithful in Christ Jesus."

> **Ephesians is the crowning glory of the New Testament.**

In Colossians 4:16, Paul refers to a letter he wrote to the Laodiceans. Since our Bible does not include an epistle to the Laodiceans, many have assumed that this Laodicean letter was lost. Many other Bible scholars, however, feel that the letter to the Laodiceans is actually this very letter, the epistle to the Ephesians. Ephesus is located not far from Laodicea in Asia Minor (modern Turkey), and it is possible that Ephesus and Laodicea were two among several cities in the region to whom this letter was addressed. This explanation may account for what would otherwise seem to be a lost letter from the apostle Paul to the Laodiceans.

The Outline of Ephesians

The theme of this epistle is a grand and exalted one, and Paul sets it forth in a way that is unique to this letter among all his letters in the New Testament. It is the theme of the nature of the true church, the body of Christ. Here is an outline of the epistle to the Ephesians:

Our Position as Christians (Ephesians 1–3)

1.	Introduction: we are redeemed by the Son, sealed by the Spirit	1
2.	Our position before God: once dead, now alive in Christ	2:1–10
3.	Our position in the church: Jews and Gentiles reconciled	2:11–22
4.	The mystery of the church revealed	3

Our Lifestyle as Christians (Ephesians 4–6)

5.	Unity in the church	4:1–6
6.	One church, many spiritual gifts	4:7–16

7.	Put off the old self, put on the new	4:17–29
8.	Do not grieve the Holy Spirit, but be filled with the Spirit	4:30–5:21
9.	Christian submission: husbands and wives, children to parents	5:22–6:4
10.	Service in the workplace	6:5–9
11.	Spiritual warfare: the armor of God, praying for boldness	6:10–20
12.	Conclusion	6:21–24

You in Christ

As we discussed in chapter 1, "Letters to the Church," the first four letters of the New Testament—Romans, 1 and 2 Corinthians, and Galatians—develop the theme "Christ in you," teaching what the indwelling life of Christ is intended to accomplish in us. But beginning with the letter to the Ephesians, the overarching theme of the epistles changes from "Christ in you" to "you in Christ." In Ephesians through Philemon, we discover what it means for us to be in Christ and to share the body life of the Lord Jesus Christ. Thus, the great theme of Ephesians is the believer in Christ and the believer in the body of Christ, the church.

Paul sets the tone for his epistle in Ephesians 1:3:

> *Praise be to the God and Father of our Lord Jesus Christ, who has blessed us in the heavenly realms with every spiritual blessing in Christ.*

It is easy to misunderstand the phrase "the heavenly realms," which appears several times in this letter. If you interpret this only as a reference to heaven after we die, you will miss the main thrust of Paul's message in Ephesians. While this phrase does include the fact that we are going to heaven someday, it speaks primarily about the life we are to live right now, here on earth. The heavenly realms are not off in some distant corner of space or on some planet or star. They are simply the realms of invisible reality in which the Christian lives right now, in contact with God and in conflict with the satanic realms in which we are all daily engaged.

The heavenly realms are the seat of Christ's authority and power. In Ephesians 2:6, we are told,

> *And God raised us up with Christ and seated us with him in the*
> *heavenly realms in Christ Jesus.*

But in the heavenly realms are also found the headquarters of the principalities and powers of evil, and the nature of our conflict with them is disclosed in Ephesians 6:12:

> *For our struggle is not against flesh and blood, but against the*
> *rulers, against the authorities, against the powers of this dark*
> *world and against the spiritual forces of evil in the heavenly realms.*

So you can see that when Paul talks about the heavenly realms, he is not talking about heaven, but about an invisible but very real realm here on earth. He is talking about a spiritual kingdom that surrounds us and constantly influences and affects us, whether for good or evil, depending upon our own choices and our relationship to these invisible powers.

The Spiritual Realms

In this realm, where every one of us lives, the apostle declares that God has already blessed us with every spiritual blessing. That is, He has given us all it takes to live in our present circumstances and relationships. Peter says the same thing in his second letter:

> *His divine power has given us everything we need for life and*
> *godliness through our knowledge of him who called us by his own*
> *glory and goodness (2 Peter 1:3).*

That means that when you receive Jesus Christ as Lord, you have already received all that God ever intends to give you. Isn't that remarkable? The weakest believers hold in their hands all that is ever possessed by the mightiest saints of God. We already have everything, because we have Christ, and in Him is every spiritual blessing and all that pertains to life and godliness. Thus, we have what it takes to live life as God intended. Any failure, therefore, is not because we are lacking anything, but *because we have not appropriated what is already ours.*

You Are the Church

Most of us have a tendency to think of the church as something we attend, something separate from us. But Paul, in this powerful letter to the Ephesians, wants us to understand that we are the church and the church is us!

Every once in a while, when I was in the pastorate, someone would come to me and say, "The church ought to do such-and-such." And I would reply, "Well, you are the church. Go do it." The person would always look at me with a bit of astonishment—and then say, "Okay, I will!" When someone would say, "The church ought to be friendlier," I would say, "All right, you and I are the church—let's be friendlier." When someone would say, "The church needs to do more to reach out to the community," I would say, "All right, you and I are the church—let's think of some things we can do to have a more effective ministry in the community." Invariably, that thought struck people as a breakthrough, a revelation—and it changed the way people lived their lives as members of the body of Christ.

The church is people. Every believer is a member of the body of Christ—the church—so I would prefer to go through this letter using the word church interchangeably with the word Christian, because every believer is a small replica of the whole church. If we understand that God lives within the church, then we must acknowledge that He also lives within each believer. Each one of us is a microcosm of the whole body. We can, therefore, go through this whole epistle relating what Paul says not to the church in some institutional sense, but to each one of us as individual believers.

> **Each believer in Jesus Christ is a microcosm of the whole body.**

The Church Is the Body

In Ephesians, Paul uses six metaphors to explain the nature of the church—and of the Christian—in relationship to Jesus Christ. In the first of these metaphors, he refers to the church as a body:

> *And God placed all things under his feet and appointed him to be head over everything for the church, which is his body, the fullness of him who fills everything in every way (1:22–23).*

The first chapter is devoted to the wonder and amazement that we as ordinary, flawed, sin-drenched human beings should be called by God in a most amazing way to become members of that body. It is a tremendous declaration! The apostle Paul never got over his amazement that he, a bowlegged, baldheaded, half-blind former persecutor of the church, should become a member of the Lord's own body, called by God before the foundation of the earth, blessed and equipped for everything that life could demand of him. That is what it means to belong to the body of Christ.

What is the purpose of the body? It is to be "the fullness of him who fills everything in every way." What a mighty phrase that is! Do you ever think of yourself that way? Do you ever dare think of yourself the way God thinks of you—as a body to be wholly filled and flooded with God Himself? If that were truly our perspective on ourselves as Christians as we go through our daily lives, I believe our lives would be transformed by that realization.

So the body of Christ is "the fullness of him who fills everything in every way." In other words, the body is the expression of the Head. Think about your own human body, which expresses and performs the desires of your head. The only time a healthy human body does not do that is when some secondary nervous center is artificially stimulated. For example, if you hit your knee in the right place with a hammer, your leg will kick up in the air without your even willing it. Even if you choose not to kick, it will react. I sometimes wonder if some of the activity of the church isn't a lot like that—an involuntary reflex action in which the body acts on its own without direction from the head.

The Church Is a Temple

Next, Paul uses the metaphor of a temple to describe the nature of the church:

> *In him the whole building is joined together and rises to become a holy temple in the Lord. And in him you too are being built together to become a dwelling in which God lives by his Spirit (2:21–22).*

When all the worthless products of human endeavor have crumbled into dust, when all the institutions and organizations we have built have been long forgotten, the temple that God is now building—His church— will be the central focus of attention through all eternity. That is what the passage implies. God is using us as His building blocks— shaping us, edging us, fitting us together, placing us in His design, using us in His plan, placing us in His temple in the place where we can be the most effective for His purpose. We are to be His temple, His house, His dwelling place, where He can enter in and say, "I'm home. This is where I am comfortable. This is where I am pleased to dwell."

> **God is using us as His building blocks.**

The Church Is a Mystery

Ephesians 3 introduces the third metaphor, where we learn that the church is a mystery, a sacred secret:

> *Although I am less than the least of all God's people, this grace was given me: to preach to the Gentiles the unsearchable riches of Christ, and to make plain to everyone the administration of this mystery, which for ages past was kept hidden in God, who created all things. His intent was that now, through the church, the manifold wisdom of God should be made known to the rulers and authorities in the heavenly realms (3:8–10).*

There are wonderful intimations here that God has had a secret plan at work through the centuries—a plan He has never unfolded to anybody—and the instrument by which He is doing it is the church. Paul is saying that, through the church, the manifold wisdom of God—all the many levels of God's knowledge and all the depths of His limitless wonders—will now be made known to all the principalities and powers that inhabit the heavenly realms.

> The purpose of the mystery of the church is to educate the universe—to make known the wisdom of God to the spiritual rulers of those invisible realms.

The purpose of the mystery of the church is to educate the universe—to make known the wisdom of God to the spiritual rulers of those invisible realms.

The Church Is a New Self

In chapter four, the apostle uses a fourth metaphor:

> *Put on the new self, created to be like God in true righteousness and holiness (4:24).*

The church is a new being, a new self with a new nature, because every Christian in it is a new self. This metaphor is linked with Paul's statement in another letter:

> *Therefore, if anyone is in Christ, he is a new creation; the old has gone, the new has come! (2 Cor. 5:17).*

> **God is building up a new generation, a new race of beings, a new order of souls or selves, the likes of which the world has never seen.**

The present creation, which began at the beginning of the heavens and the earth, has long since grown old and is passing away. The world with all its wealth and its wisdom belongs to that which is passing. But God is building up a new generation, a new race of beings, a new order of souls or selves, the likes of which the world has never seen. It is a generation that is even better than Adam, better than the original creation—it is a new creation!

In Romans, we learned that all we lost in Adam has been regained in Christ—and more!

> *For if, by the trespass of the one man, death reigned through that one man, how much more will those who receive God's abundant provision of grace and of the gift of righteousness reign in life through the one man, Jesus Christ (Rom. 5:17).*

Paul says that the whole creation "waits in eager anticipation" ("is standing on tiptoe," for that is the literal meaning), craning its neck to see the manifestation of the sons of God, the day of the unveiling of this new creation (see Rom. 8:19).

But remember, this new creation is being made right now, and you are invited to put on this new self, moment by moment, day by day, in order that you might meet the pressures and problems of life in the world today. That is why the church is here. The church is a new self, and the purpose of the new self is to exercise a new ministry. In this same chapter of Ephesians, we read,

> *But to each one of us grace has been given as Christ apportioned it (4:7).*

This new self in each of us has been given a gift (that is what is meant by the word *grace* in this verse) that we never had before we became Christians. Our task is to discover and exercise that gift. When the church falters and fails and loses its direction, it's because Christians have lost this great truth, and the gifts He has given us have gone undiscovered and unused.

The risen Lord has given a gift to you, just as the lord in the parable gave the talents to each of his servants, entrusting them with his property until his return (see Matt. 25). When our Lord comes back, His judgment will be based on what you did with the gift He gave to you.

The Church Is a Bride

Ephesians 5 introduces another metaphor to describe the true nature of the church: The church is a bride:

> Husbands, love your wives, just as Christ loved the church and gave himself up for her to make her holy, cleansing her by the washing with water through the word, and to present her to himself as a radiant church, without stain or wrinkle or any other blemish, but holy and blameless (vv. 25–27).

And then Paul quotes the words of God in Genesis:

> "For this reason a man will leave his father and mother and be united to his wife, and the two will become one flesh." This is a profound mystery—but I am talking about Christ and the church (Eph. 5:31–32).

The church is a bride, and Paul says Christ's intention in preparing the church as a bride is that He might present the church to Himself. Isn't that what every bridegroom desires—that his bride shall be his and his alone? During their early days of courtship she may go out with some other fellows, but when they are engaged she has promised to be his and they are both waiting for the day when that can be fully, finally realized. Then at last the day comes when they stand before the marriage altar and promise to love, honor, and cherish one another until death shall part them. They then become each other's—she is his and he is hers, for the enjoyment of each other throughout their lifetime together. That is a picture both of the church and of the Christian in relation to Christ, the bridegroom.

Do you ever think of yourself this way? My own devotional life was revolutionized when it dawned on me that the Lord Jesus was looking forward to our time together. If I missed our time together, He was disappointed! I realized that not only was I receiving from Him, but that He was receiving from me, and that He longed and yearned for me. When I met with the Lord after that, it was with a new sense that He loved me and delighted in our time of fellowship.

The Church Is a Soldier

The last metaphor of the church that Paul paints in the epistle to the Ephesians is the metaphor of a soldier:

> *Therefore put on the full armor of God, so that when the day of evil comes, you may be able to stand your ground, and after you have done everything, to stand. Stand firm then, with the belt of truth buckled around your waist, with the breastplate of righteousness in place, and with your feet fitted with the readiness that comes from the gospel of peace. In addition to all this, take up the shield of faith, with which you can extinguish all the flaming arrows of the evil one. Take the helmet of salvation and the sword of the Spirit, which is the word of God (6:13–17).*

What is the purpose of a soldier? To fight battles! And that is what God is doing in us and through us right now. He has given us the great privilege of serving on the battlefield upon which His great victories are won.

In fact, there is actually a very real sense in which we are the battlefield! That is the essence of the story of Job. This man who dearly loved God was struck without warning by a series of tragedies. All in one day, he lost everything that mattered to him, everything he prized, even his entire family except his wife. Job didn't understand what was happening, but God had chosen him to be the battlefield for a conflict with Satan. God allowed Satan to afflict Job physically, mentally, and materially, because God knew that Job was the perfect battleground upon which to win a mighty victory against the great invisible powers of the heavenly realms. Job was a soldier in a great spiritual battle—and so are we.

We are soldiers in a great spiritual battle.

In his first letter, the apostle John writes to his young Christian friends:

> *I write to you, young men, because you are strong, and the word of God lives in you, and you have overcome the evil one (1 John 2:14).*

In other words, John is telling his young friends, "You have learned how to fight, how to move out as soldiers in a spiritual war, how to throw off the confusing restraints of the world, how not to be conformed to the age in which you live, how to move against the tide of the culture—and in so doing you have overcome Satan and you have glorified God!"

I love the story of Daniel who, as a teenager, was a prisoner in a foreign land. He was trapped in a pagan culture and had to fight the battle day by day, counting solely upon God's faithfulness to defend him when everything was against him. The pressures brought to bear upon him were incredible. Yet Daniel met the tests again and again. He won the battle, defeated Satan, and gave God the glory. In a tremendous spiritual battle, Daniel was a faithful soldier.

This is the privilege to which God is calling us in this day of world unrest and increasing darkness. This is the battle God calls us to as our world slips closer and closer to the mother of all battles, Armageddon. God is calling us to be soldiers, to walk in the steps of those who have won the battle before us. They have shown us how to remain faithful, even unto death. Battered, bruised, and bloodied, they have counted it a badge of honor to serve in God's army, to be wounded in service to the King.

> God is calling us to walk in the steps of those who have won the battle before us—those who have been faithful unto death.

This, then, is our six-fold calling. God has equipped us with every spiritual blessing, with every gift we need, so that we might become a body, a temple, a mystery, a new self, a bride, and a soldier for Jesus Christ. That is quite a calling!

The ultimate exhortation of this letter is found in Ephesians 4:1, where Paul writes,

As a prisoner for the Lord, then, I urge you to live a life worthy of the calling you have received.

Ephesians gives us an exalted picture—a series of pictures, in fact—to reveal to us the grandeur of the church in God's plan and the crucial importance of every believer in God's sight. Never lose sight of what God is doing through you, through the church. The world cannot see it, because the world is unaware of the heavenly realms. The world has no idea what is taking place through you and me, through the church. But you know what God is doing through you. His power surges through you. His love for the world flows out of you. His courage for the battle emboldens you. So do not lose heart. There's a war on—and you are on the winning side!

NOTES

NOTES

ADVENTURING
through
PAUL'S EPISTLES

CHAPTER SEVEN

PHILIPPIANS:
CHRIST, OUR
CONFIDENCE
and STRENGTH

THE LETTER TO THE PHILIPPIANS has been called the tenderest of all Paul's letters. It is also the most delightful to read. It brims over with expressions of praise, confidence, and rejoicing, despite the fact that this is one of Paul's prison epistles, written during his confinement in Rome.

We find the background for this letter in Acts 16, which tells of Paul's visit to Philippi and the founding of the Philippian church, and in Acts 28, which tells the story of Paul's house arrest in Rome.

> **Philippians brims over with expressions of praise, confidence, and rejoicing.**

The founding of the Philippian church took place during the exciting and danger-filled days when Paul and Silas journeyed together on the second missionary journey. Arriving in Philippi, they first met a group of women having a prayer meeting by the riverside, and they shared the gospel with these women. One of them, Lydia, a seller of purple goods (one who dyed garments for royalty and the wealthy), invited Paul and Silas into her home. Throughout the centuries, Lydia's name has been known because of her kindness and hospitality to the apostle Paul, and the Philippian church had its beginning in her home.

Paul's preaching throughout the city stirred up quite a reaction. It aroused the resentment of the rulers, who had Paul and Silas arrested and flogged, then thrown into jail and fastened in stocks. That same night, as Paul and Silas were praying and singing hymns to God and the other prisoners were listening to them, an earthquake struck—a quake so violent that the foundations of the prison crumbled. The prison doors flew open, and all the prisoners' chains came loose. The jailer, seeing that all the prisoners were free to escape, pulled his sword and would have fallen upon it when Paul shouted, "Don't harm yourself! We're all here!"

The jailer rushed in, fell at the feet of the two missionaries, and asked, "What must I do to be saved?"

"Believe in the Lord Jesus," they replied, "and you will be saved—you and your household."

Paul later went on to the cities of Thessalonica, Berea, Athens, Corinth, and other places in Greece.

Years later, finding himself a prisoner of the Emperor Nero in Rome, Paul thought back on his beloved friends in the church he had founded at Philippi, and he wrote them a letter, the epistle to the Philippians. Although he was allowed to stay in his own rented house as he awaited his trial before the emperor, Paul was chained day and night to a Roman soldier. He knew that he possibly faced a death sentence, yet this epistle glows with radiance and joy, confidence and strength.

If you are going through times of pressure and trial, I urge you to read this little letter. It will encourage you greatly, especially if you remember the circumstances out of which it was written.

> **If you are going through times of pressure and trial, I urge you to read this little letter.**

The Outline of Philippians

Philippians is divided into four chapters, which represent four natural divisions within the text. One of the abiding frustrations of many Bible teachers is the arbitrariness of the chapter divisions throughout Scripture. These divisions, of course, were not part of the original Scripture text but were added much later. In many passages of Scripture, chapter divisions are inserted in the middle of a thought, thus obstructing the flow of the writer's argument. But amazingly, the chapter divisions in Philippians all make excellent sense and help to organize the message of this encouraging and instructive New Testament book.

Here's an overview of Paul's epistle to the Philippians:

Christ Our Life (Philippians 1)

1. Paul's thankfulness that his afflictions serve to spread the gospel — 1:1–26
2. Paul encourages others who are afflicted — 1:27–30

Christ Our Example (Philippians 2)

3. Christ, our example for humility — 2:1–16
4. Paul's example of humility — 2:17–18
5. Timothy's example of humility — 2:19–24
6. Epaphroditus's example of humility — 2:25–30

Christ Our Confidence (Philippians 3)

7. Do not place confidence in the flesh — 3:1–9
8. Christ is the source of our confidence — 3:10–16
9. Do not live for the flesh — 3:17–21

Christ Our Energizer (Philippians 4)

10. Seek peace and unity in the strength of the Lord — 4:1–3

The overall theme of this letter is Jesus Christ's availability to us for the problems of life. The church at Philippi was not troubled by serious doctrinal or behavioral problems like some of the other churches. It experienced only the normal problems of everyday life—Christians who have trouble getting along with each other, growing pains, ministry stresses, disturbances by certain persons whose beliefs and practices were not in full accord with the true Christian faith.

To deal with these problems, Paul designed this epistle as a guide for ordinary living. The recurring refrain throughout the letter is one of joy and rejoicing. Repeatedly the apostle uses phrases such as, "rejoice," "rejoice with me," "rejoice in the Lord." Rejoice in your sufferings, rejoice in your afflictions. This becomes, then, a letter in which we are instructed how to live victoriously and joyously in the midst of the normal difficulties of life.

Christ Our Life

The themes of Philippians are captured in four key verses, the first of which is found in Philippians 1:21:

> For to me, to live is Christ and to die is gain.

I think we often treat this verse as a statement of Christian escapism. We put the emphasis at the end of the sentence, "to die is gain," and we think, *Yes, it would be great to get away from all the pressures and pain and struggles of life.* But that's not what Paul is saying. Look closely and you see that he is really saying, "I don't know which to choose. To me to live is to have Christ, but on the other hand, to die is to gain heaven. I enjoy living the adventure of life, but I long to experience the next adventure in the life to come." Paul was certainly not fed up with life. He loved living, because he wanted Christ to have every opportunity to live through him.

How could Paul be so excited about life when he was forced to live it under prison conditions? Because he saw what God was doing through him even while he was in chains. A unique evangelistic enterprise was occurring in Rome, the like of which may never have been seen before or since. And Paul—chains, guards, house arrest, and all—was at the hub of this evangelistic enterprise. God had a plan for reaching the Roman Empire. And do you know who God placed in charge of all the arrangements for this great evangelistic outreach in Rome? Emperor Nero! As Paul himself explains,

> **How could Paul be so excited about life when he was forced to live it under prison conditions?**

It has become clear throughout the whole palace guard and to everyone else that I am in chains for Christ (1:13).

If you read between the lines, you can see what was happening. Nero, the emperor, had commanded that every six hours one of the finest young men in the whole Roman Empire, from the elite who constituted his personal bodyguard, would be brought in and chained to the apostle Paul. Nero's purpose was to keep a fresh guard on this dangerous man. But God had a higher purpose, and He used Nero to send a succession of Rome's best and brightest to be instructed by Paul in the things of Christ!

Isn't that amazing? One by one these young men were coming to Christ because they could see the reality of Jesus Christ living through this amazing man, Paul. If you doubt that, look at the last chapter of the letter, where in the next to last verse Paul says:

All the saints send you greetings, especially those who belong to Caesar's household (4:22).

No human mind could have conceived such a unique plan for evangelizing the Roman Empire! But that is the kind of God Paul served, and that is why he could say, "To me, to live is Christ. I don't know what He is going to do next but whatever it is, it will be interesting and exciting!" That is what life in Christ means.

Christ Our Example

In chapter 2, Paul deals with the problem of disunity that was threatening some of the saints at Philippi. Certain individuals were quarreling, and there were divisions within the church. This is constantly happening, in one way or another, in most churches. People get irritated with each other; they get upset over the way other people do things. They do not like someone's attitude or tone of voice. Then cliques and divisions, which are always destructive to the life and vitality of a church, begin to develop. So Paul points out to these people that Christ is our example in settling difficulties and problems. The key passage in this section is verse 5:

Your attitude should be the same as that of Christ Jesus.

Then he immediately proceeds to explain what the attitude of Jesus, the mind of Christ, was like:

Who, being in very nature God, did not consider equality with God something to be grasped, but made himself nothing, taking the very nature of a servant, being made in human likeness. And being found in appearance as a man, he humbled himself and became obedient to death—even death on a cross! (2:6–8).

That was the self-condescension of Jesus Christ. It was the emptying out of all that He held of value in His life. This, says Paul, is the mind of Jesus Christ. In your disagreements with one another, have this attitude toward each other: Do not hang onto your rights at all costs. How apropos this is in these days when we hear so often about insisting on our rights. How different is Christ's example!

Dr. H. A. Ironside used to tell a story that took place when he was only nine or ten years old. His mother took him to a church business meeting, which at some point erupted into a quarrel between two men. One of them stood and pounded the desk, saying, "All I want is my rights."

Sitting nearby was an old Scotsman, somewhat hard of hearing, who cupped his hand behind his ear and said, "Aye, brother, what's that you say? What do you want?"

The angry gentleman replied, "I just said that all I want is my rights, that's all!"

The old Scot snorted, "Your rights, brother? Is that what you want, your rights? Well, I say if you had your rights, you'd be in hell. The Lord Jesus Christ didn't come to get His rights, He came to get His wrongs. And He got 'em."

The fellow who had been bickering stood transfixed for a moment, then abruptly sat down and said, "You're right. Settle it any way you like."

In a few moments the argument was settled—and it was settled when the combatants were challenged to take on the mind of Christ, the attitude of the One who never demanded His rights but who, uncomplaining, took His wrongs, humbling Himself, becoming obedient to death, even the death of the cross.

But don't stop there. What was the result of Jesus' self-effacing humility and sacrifice?

> God exalted him to the highest place and gave him the name that is above every name, that at the name of Jesus every knee should bow, in heaven and on earth and under the earth, and every tongue confess that Jesus Christ is Lord, to the glory of God the Father (2:9–11).

When Jesus willingly surrendered His rights, God gave Him every right in the universe. Jesus placed everything He had, everything He treasured, in the hands of God the Father, and the result was that God the Father vindicated Him. This is what Paul is saying to quarreling Christians: Give up your rights. Don't insist on them. With Christ as your example, lay aside your rights and absorb your wrongs. Replace selfishness with humility, and trust God to vindicate you. That is the mind of Christ. And if we would truly put that admonition into practice, we would be different people. There would be no quarreling within churches and no divisions among Christians if we all truly followed Christ our example and patterned our minds after His.

> **Replace selfishness with humility, and trust God to vindicate you. That is the mind of Christ.**

Christ Our Confidence

Chapter 3 sets forth Christ our confidence, our motivating power. He is the One who moves us to boldly, obediently step out in faith, believing that we can achieve the task God has set for us. And isn't that what most of us lack and what is in such short supply today?

Everywhere we look, we see books, tapes, and seminars offering us a motivational boost, advertising that they can build our confidence so that we can achieve our goals. Yet if we truly understood what it means to be in Christ and to have Christ living in us, we would possess all the confidence and motivation we need to achieve any godly goal. What more confidence do we need than to have the Creator of the universe living within us and empowering all we do? What greater motivation could we possess than to know that Jesus is on our side, and that with Him as our encourager and our coach, there's no way we can lose!

All that is lacking in us is the true knowledge of what we already possess in Christ. That is why Paul says, in Philippians 3:10:

> *I want to know Christ and the power of his resurrection and the fellowship of sharing in his sufferings, becoming like him in his death.*

The power of Christ our confidence stands in stark contrast to the power of self.

The power of Christ our confidence stands in contrast to the power of the self—in which most of us place our confidence. In Philippians 3:3, Paul defines a Christian as one who worships by the Spirit of God, who glories in Christ Jesus not in the self, and who puts no confidence in the flesh, in human pride and power. Compare that statement with all the best-selling books and late-night infomercials that try to get us to discover the power within us, trying to build up our confidence in our own minds and our own flesh.

If anyone had the right to glory in the flesh, it was the apostle Paul.

> *I myself have reasons for such confidence.*
> *If anyone else thinks he has reasons to put confidence in the flesh, I have more: circumcised on the eighth day, of the people of Israel, of the tribe of Benjamin, a Hebrew of Hebrews; in regard to the law, a Pharisee; as for zeal, persecuting the church; as for legalistic righteousness, faultless (3:4–6).*

What a lot of reasons to have confidence and pride in his own flesh! Perfect ancestry, as purebred and highborn as they come; perfect ritual and religious observance; perfect religious zeal and morality; perfect performance in the strictest sect of the Hebrew religion! Yet despite all these reasons for human pride, Paul counted them as worthless next to the confidence that Jesus Christ gives. In verse 7, he writes,

> *Whatever was to my profit I now consider loss for the sake of Christ.*

Christ Our Energizer

You've seen him a thousand times: The pink Energizer bunny, with the big drum in front of him and the Energizer batteries on his back, and "He keeps going and going and going. . . ." In Philippians 4, Paul tells us that we are like that little pink bunny! With Christ living in us, energizing us and empowering us, we can keep going and going and going in service to Him, fulfilling His will, reaching out to people in His name.

I can think of few things more frustrating than to have a great desire but not the ability to fulfill it. In Philippians 4, Paul tells us that God not only gives us the desire to live our lives in service to Him and others, but He also supplies us with the strength and energy so that we have the power to fulfill that desire. Paul speaks directly to that with this great declaration that has been such an inspiration to believers down through the centuries:

I can do everything through him who gives me strength (4:13).

Is this statement mere wishful thinking or idealism on the apostle's part? Or is it a practical, reliable truth?

Practical! Absolutely practical! In fact, just to show how practical and trustworthy Christ's energizing power is in our everyday lives, Paul addresses one of the most common problems in the church—the problem of getting along with others. Two members of the Philippian church, Euodia and Syntyche, were obviously involved in some kind of a disagreement, and the apostle Paul begs them to end their disagreement and be of the same mind in the Lord.

Is Paul asking the impossible? No! As he says in verse 13: "I can do everything through him who gives me strength." Even put up with odious people? Positively! Even get along with touchy people? Absolutely! When Christ is our energizer, we can get along with people, and we can keep going and going and going along with them, loving them, accepting them, and forgiving them for the sake of the unity of the body of Christ.

Next, Paul addresses the matter of worry. In Philippians 4:6–7, Paul—a man with every rightful reason to worry, a man in chains, a man facing a possible death sentence from Rome's erratic ruler, Nero—writes:

Do not be anxious about anything, but in everything, by prayer and petition, with thanksgiving, present your requests to God. And the peace of God, which transcends all understanding, will guard your hearts and your minds in Christ Jesus.

What a recipe for mental peace and serenity! Paul is not minimizing worries and problems and the cares of life. He is simply telling us not to be ruled by them. He doesn't suggest that we live in denial and try to suppress our anxieties and pretend they aren't there. He is saying that we should present those anxieties to the Lord and allow the Lord to give us His peace—a peace beyond our ability to understand. We don't know where that peace comes from or how it works, but believer after believer can tell you it is real.

I can personally testify to many times in my own life when I was low or worried or fearful; yet after sharing those feelings with God, I felt my soul suddenly flooded with peace and a sense of well-being in the Lord. Here again, it is a case of the Lord Jesus Christ's energizing power flooding our lives with His strength, enabling us to keep going and going and going, even amid our fears and worries.

Finally there is the matter of poverty and material blessing. Paul has known both, and he wants to convey to the Philippian Christians—and to you and me—what a Christlike attitude toward these conditions should be:

> *I am not saying this because I am in need, for I have learned to be content whatever the circumstances. I know what it is to be in need, and I know what it is to have plenty. I have learned the secret of being content in any and every situation, whether well fed or hungry, whether living in plenty or in want (4:11–12).*

What is Paul's secret of contentment? In verse 19, he passes that secret on to the Philippians and to us:

> *And my God will meet all your needs according to his glorious riches in Christ Jesus.*

Paul's Secret of Contentment

Our Lord Jesus Christ, our strength, our energizer, will supply all our need, enabling us to keep going and going and going.

The letter to the Philippians embodies the soul and the life secrets of a man who ran the full course, who fought the good fight, who kept the faith, who kept going and going for God. This little power-packed book contains Paul's road map for a life lived with power, enthusiasm, and a sense of adventure. And the same One who lived through Paul also lives through us. Christ is our life; Christ is our example; Christ is our confidence; Christ is our energizer and our strength.

NOTES

NOTES

NOTES

ADVENTURING
through
PAUL'S EPISTLES

CHAPTER EIGHT

COLOSSIANS:
POWER *and* JOY!

PAUL WROTE MOST OF HIS LETTERS to churches that he himself
founded. He did not establish the church at Rome, however, nor the church
at Colossae, in Greece, to which this letter was written. We can't verify who
established the church at Colossae, but it likely was Epaphroditus (also known
as Epaphras), a man mentioned in some of Paul's other letters. This letter
mentions that he was from Colossae. We also don't know where Epaphroditus
heard the gospel, but after hearing and believing, he apparently took the gospel back to his hometown, where he began to proclaim Christ. The church to
which this letter was written was likely the result of the bold hometown witness of Epaphroditus, and these believers had never met Paul face-to-face.

Colossians, Philippians, and Ephesians were written at about the same
time, during Paul's first imprisonment, and are therefore called the Prison
Epistles. Notice that the structure and content of this letter are similar to
Paul's letter to the Ephesians.

The Outline of Colossians

Christ, the Head of Creation and the Head of the Church (Colossians 1–2)

1.	Introduction and prayer for the Colossians	1:1–14
2.	Christ, the Head of creation	1:15–17
3.	Christ, the Head of the church	1:18–2:3
4.	Our freedom in Christ	2:4–23

Submission to Christ the Head (Colossians 3–4)

5.	Put off the old self	3:1–11
6.	Put on the new self	3:12–4:6
7.	Conclusion	4:7–18

Jesus the Firstborn

The Christians at Colossae had a problem, and that is Paul's focus in this
letter. They were on the verge of losing their understanding of the power
by which the Christian life is lived, and this letter is Paul's great explanation of the power and joy that God provides for living the Christian life.
Paul expresses the theme of Colossians in his introductory prayer:

> *We pray this in order that you may live a life worthy of the Lord*
> *and may please him in every way: bearing fruit in every good*
> *work, growing in the knowledge of God, being strengthened with*
> *all power according to his glorious might so that you may have*

great endurance and patience, and joyfully giving thanks to the Father, who has qualified you to share in the inheritance of the saints in the kingdom of light (1:10–12).

Paul's prayer is that Christians *might be strengthened with all power* (that's why he wrote the letter) *according to God's glorious might* (the central issue of this letter). Beginning on this note, Paul then sets forth the power in the Christian life: Jesus Christ. How can Jesus—a man who was born as a baby, lived as a man, and died on a cross—be the source of all power? Simple. Jesus is God. Paul makes this point in a powerful way in verses 15–20:

> **The source of all power in the Christian life is Jesus Christ.**

He is the image of the invisible God, the firstborn over all creation. For by him all things were created: things in heaven and on earth, visible and invisible, whether thrones or powers or rulers or authorities; all things were created by him and for him. He is before all things, and in him all things hold together. And he is the head of the body, the church; he is the beginning and the firstborn from among the dead, so that in everything he might have the supremacy. For God was pleased to have all his fullness dwell in him, and through him to reconcile to himself all things, whether things on earth or things in heaven, by making peace through his blood, shed on the cross.

Anyone who claims that Jesus is not truly God has at least two big problems. One is the gospel of John, a book entirely devoted to the subject of the deity of Christ. The other is this passage, which is an absolutely clear and unambiguous statement of the deity of Christ. Of course, the deity of Christ is a theme that is woven throughout Scripture, but John and Colossians make the case in terms that are direct and unassailable.

Twice in Colossians 1, Paul refers to Jesus as the firstborn. *Firstborn* is a term that confuses some people. It does not mean, as some people have understood it, that Jesus had a beginning—that He is not truly eternal. Here, the word firstborn refers not to the chronology of Jesus Christ but to His role or position. In the culture to which Colossians was written, firstborn was understood to mean the heir, the first in line as the owner or master. This phrase, "firstborn over all creation," means that the Lord Jesus stands in relationship to all creation just as an heir stands in relationship to a parent's property. Jesus is not part of the created order. Rather, He owns it and rules it as the heir of the Father.

In this passage, Paul declares Jesus Christ to be the Creator, the One who brought all the worlds into being with a word, the One who, being God the Son, was present in the beginning with God the Father. Note Paul's statement in verse 17:

He is before all things, and in him all things hold together.

One of the continuing puzzles of science is the question of what holds the universe together. We know that everything is made up of tiny atoms that consist of electrons buzzing around a nucleus. Why doesn't the centrifugal force of those orbiting electrons cause atoms to fly apart? Scientists talk hopefully of a "grand unified theory" of forces that they hope will someday explain what holds the universe together, but science can only point to unnamed, undiscovered, unknown forces.

The predicament of science in its pursuit of the unknown force reminds me of Paul's experience in Athens where he encountered an altar to "AN UNKNOWN GOD." It is the "unknown God" that science is struggling with today. But He is not unknown. His name is Jesus of Nazareth, and He is the Grand Unifying Force of the universe. All power in the natural world comes from Him; He is before all things, and in Him all things hold together.

> **Jesus of Nazareth is the Grand Unifying Force of the universe . . . in Him all things hold together.**

In verse 18, Paul goes on to say that the One who created the universe and holds it together is also the One who created the church and holds it together:

He is the head of the body, the church; he is the beginning and the firstborn from among the dead, so that in everything he might have the supremacy.

Notice, again, that term *firstborn*. Jesus, says Paul, is "the firstborn from among the dead." What does that mean? First, it does not mean that Jesus was the first person ever to be raised from the dead, because Scripture records others who preceded Him. In fact, Jesus Himself raised some of them. What Paul means is that Jesus is the heir, the Lord of all the new creation. He is the Head of the new creation, as the apostle tells us, and we are part of a new body, the new body of men and women that

God is forming—a body called the church. Jesus is the Head of that body, and from Him flows all power—the power He demonstrated on the first Easter: *resurrection power.*

I am becoming increasingly convinced that the problem with most Christians is that we do not understand what the Bible teaches about resurrection power. If we had any idea what this power is and how it functions, we would never again live as we live now.

> The problem with most Christians is that we do not understand what the Bible teaches about resurrection power.

Resurrection power is quiet. It is the kind of power that was evident in the Lord Jesus. He came silently from the tomb—no sound effects, no pyrotechnic visual effects. There was only the quiet, inexorable, irresistible power of a risen life. The stone was rolled away—not to let Jesus out but to let people in, so they could see that the tomb was empty.

This is the same power that God has released to us. His quiet but irresistible power changes hearts and lives and attitudes, recreating from within. That is resurrection power. It flows to us from the Head of the new creation, the risen Christ, the source of all power.

Christ in You, the Hope of Glory

Next, Paul goes on to show for whom God intends this power:

> *Once you were alienated from God and were enemies in your minds because of your evil behavior. But now he has reconciled you by Christ's physical body through death to present you holy in his sight, without blemish and free from accusation (1:21–22).*

In this passage, Paul is addressing you and me, as well as the Colossians. We too were once estranged, enemies of God because of sin; but now God has reconciled us through the physical death of Jesus, unleashing His resurrection power in order to make us holy and guiltless in His sight. Then Paul goes on to give us a demonstration of this power in his own life. He says that God called him and put him in the ministry to proclaim a mystery:

> *I have become its servant by the commission God gave me to present to you the word of God in its fullness—the mystery that has been kept hidden for ages and generations, but is now disclosed to the saints. To them God has chosen to make known among the*

Gentiles the glorious riches of this mystery, which is Christ in you, the hope of glory (1:25–27).

In other words, you will not find this mystery explained in the Old Testament. It was experienced there but never explained. Now, however, it has been disclosed to the saints, to the followers of Jesus Christ. What is this mystery? "Christ in you, the hope of glory."

Christ living in you—this is the supreme declaration of the Christian church. You have never preached the gospel until you have told people not only that their sins will be forgiven when they come to Christ, but that Jesus Himself will indwell them and empower them! That is the transforming power of the gospel: Jesus lives in us and through us, giving us the creation power, the resurrection power, to do all God expects us to do and all He designed us to do and all He created us to do.

> Christ living in you—this is the supreme declaration of the Christian church.

Jesus died for us so that He might live in us. That is the ultimate glory of the Christian gospel.

Plugged into the Source

Paul goes on to describe what it means to live by the power of Christ. In Colossians 1:28–29, he writes:

We proclaim him, admonishing and teaching everyone with all wisdom, so that we may present everyone perfect in Christ. To this end I labor, struggling with all his energy, which so powerfully works in me.

What does Paul mean when he talks about "struggling with all his energy, which so powerfully works in me"? Well, just think about the life that Paul lived and the work that he accomplished. Think of this amazing apostle, with his indefatigable journeying night and day, through shipwreck and hardship of every kind, working with his hands, enduring persecution, stonings, beatings, and opposition as he carried the gospel from one end of the Roman Empire to the other. Some of us think that we can barely make it from weekend to weekend in our 9-to-5 jobs. But this man was spending himself day and night, seven days a week, for the sake of Jesus Christ. He could not do that in his own strength, his own energy. He plugged into an outside power source, the ultimate power source, and he allowed that power to surge through him, performing the will of God.

In other words, Christ in you! The hope of glory!

If Christians would only understand the power that God has made available to us, we would never again be the same. We would never have to plead with people in the church to perform needed ministries or roles. We would never have a shortage of workers for our neighborhood ministries, or of people to act as advisors on youth mission trips. We would never have a shortage of Sunday school teachers, Bible-study leaders, youth advisors, or visitation volunteers. We would not be giving the excuse, "Oh, I just don't have the strength to do it. I don't have the energy," because we all have the energy available to us. The source is Christ, the extension cord is the Holy Spirit, and we are the little electrical appliances that God wants to enliven with His resurrection power and to use according to His eternal plan.

> If Christians would only understand the power that God has made available to us, we would never again be the same.

Hidden Treasures of Wisdom and Knowledge

And there are even more depths to this mystery of Christ. He is not only the source of energy, but the source of understanding, wisdom, and knowledge. In chapter 2, Paul continues his exploration of the mystery of Christ:

> *My purpose is that they may be encouraged in heart and united in love, so that they may have the full riches of complete understanding, in order that they may know the mystery of God, namely, Christ, in whom are hidden all the treasures of wisdom and knowledge (2:2–3).*

Paul also warns about certain false powers that would woo us away from the true power that Christ has given us. These warnings are as valid and relevant today as they were when he wrote them. More than ever before, people today are in search of power—power to achieve goals, wealth, status, success. Thousands of people are spending millions of dollars dialing up psychic hotlines, buying videotape series, or going to seminars that are actually high-pressure sales pitches—all in search of the power to get what they want or to become their idealized self. All that searching for false power when the true Power is immediately available in the person of Jesus Christ.

If Jesus lives in us, we don't need any more power than we already possess. We don't need more of Jesus; He just needs more of us. Now that we have the power, our job is to live by that power on a daily basis. As Paul tells us in 2:6–7,

Just as you received Christ Jesus as Lord, continue to live in him, rooted and built up in him, strengthened in the faith as you were taught, and overflowing with thankfulness.

False Sources of Power

It is not enough simply to receive Jesus. We must live in Him. When we do, an attitude of thankfulness permeates our lives. To look at some Christians, you would think that our Bibles translate this verse "overflowing with grumbling." But Paul underscores the need for thankfulness in our lives. What robs us of a spirit of thankfulness? Primarily, it's the idea that power comes from human knowledge, as Paul shows us in verse 8:

See to it that no one takes you captive through hollow and deceptive philosophy, which depends on human tradition and the basic principles of this world rather than on Christ.

I have seen this principle tragically played out in so many lives. I have seen young people from Christian homes—full of faith and enthusiasm— go into a college or university and come out with their faith destroyed, their enthusiasm turned to cynicism. Why? Because they have been exposed to the wily, subtle teachings of human wisdom. No one warned them—or perhaps they ignored the warnings they received—about the deceitfulness of this world's wisdom. They fell prey to human knowledge.

False Power Source #1: Human Knowledge

This statement may seem to imply that the gospel is anti-intellectual. But the Bible is not against knowledge. It is against knowledge that does not come under the judgment of God's Word. Certainly not all of the knowledge of this world is false knowledge. Much of it is good and true and cannot be found in Scripture: for example, medical knowledge and techniques of surgery; technical knowledge such as how to build a computer or a space shuttle; historical knowledge such as the defeat of Napoleon at Waterloo or events of the Civil War. All of this is human knowledge, and it is valuable.

But Paul wants us to understand that there is a deceptive knowledge that comes from false sources—traditions and philosophies that have built up, idea upon idea, over the centuries. Many of these traditions and philosophies mingle truth and error in such a way that the two become indistinguishable. Those who accept these ideas uncritically are bound to accept as much error as they do truth. It will lead them, therefore, into mistaken concepts and erroneous and injurious ideas, such as: "The human spirit is recycled again and again through reincarnation." Or, "As a human being, you have totally unlimited power and potential to be your own god, to make up your own morality." Or, "A human being is just a mound of molecules that is born, lives, and dies—there is no afterlife, no purpose for living, so enjoy yourself, forget faith and morality, eat, drink, and be merry for this moment, because that's all there is." These philosophies are prevalent today, and all are false—completely contrary to the true knowledge of Scripture. They depend, as Paul says, "on human tradition."

But Paul goes on to say that there is also deceptive knowledge that is built on "the basic principles of this world rather than on Christ." What does he mean? Paul is referring here to the dark powers that (as he brings out in other letters) rule this world, govern the minds of men and women, darken the human intellect, and lead human beings into self-destructive error. Much of what human beings consider to be "knowledge" is actually demonic deception.

Human knowledge, then, is rudimentary, elementary, and basic to the fallen nature of this world. It stays on the periphery of truth, never getting to the real heart of spiritual reality. That is why our nation's university community, its entertainment community, its information and news community, and its political establishment have become so saturated with those who profess the highest levels of human knowledge yet are filled with vileness, corruption, immorality, lawlessness, drug abuse, and every evidence of moral decay and spiritual deterioration. Today, all of these institutions in our society are permeated—if not dominated—by a philosophy called deconstructionism, a worldly philosophy that teaches that words have no objective content, and therefore words have no truth.

Today's liberal theology has become deeply infected with the disease of deconstructionism, and it fosters two very destructive beliefs: First, *if truth cannot be assigned to words, then we can make words mean anything we want them to*. We no longer have to be concerned with objective truth, with true truth. Each of us can invent our own truth, our own reality. I can lie and call it truth if it gets me what I want. Second, *the Bible—the Word, or Logos of God—can be deconstructed, emptied of all truth*. These words of Jesus make no sense to deconstructionists: "Sanctify them by the truth; your word is truth" (John 17:17). While Jesus says God's Logos is truth, the wisdom of this world cancels out the Logos of God, portraying the Word of God as empty and meaningless. "You have your truth," says the wisdom of this world, "and I have my truth—so don't you dare impose your truth on me!"

Even at its truest and most pure, human knowledge does not address the heart of reality as the Word of God does. The truth of this world, when it is validated by God's Word, can complement the truth of Scripture (as when archaeological discoveries verify biblical accounts). But human knowledge can never supersede, contradict, or invalidate God's Word. The wisdom of God always stands above any so-called knowledge of this world.

False Power Source #2: Religious Substitutes

Paul goes on to warn about a second false source of power, which also leads many people astray:

> *Do not let anyone judge you by what you eat or drink, or with regard to a religious festival, a New Moon celebration or a Sabbath day. These are a shadow of the things that were to come; the reality, however, is found in Christ. . . .*
>
> *Since you died with Christ to the basic principles of this world, why, as though you still belonged to it, do you submit to its rules: "Do not handle! Do not taste! Do not touch!"? These are all destined to perish with use, because they are based on human commands and teachings (2:16–17, 20–22).*

What is this false source of power? It is found under many names: unrestrained zeal, legalism, religious extremism, judgmentalism, pharisaism. This false source of power manifests itself in the keeping of days and special feasts and regulations and ascetic practices—flogging the body, wearing a hair shirt, laboring long hours out of zeal for the cause. Such practices may look like sources of spiritual power, but, says the apostle, they are not.

> *Such regulations indeed have an appearance of wisdom, with their self-imposed worship, their false humility and their harsh treatment of the body, but they lack any value in restraining sensual indulgence (2:23).*

You see, you can wear an outfit made of burlap and be filled with lust. You can beat your body black and blue and still be guilty of lascivious thinking. These outward legalistic, ascetic trappings provide no check to the indulgence of the flesh. Therefore, they do not generate the power to lead the kind of life that we must live.

False Power Source #3: Satanic Substitutes

Finally, Paul mentions a third source of false power—one of the most deceptive sources of all!

Do not let anyone who delights in false humility and the worship of angels disqualify you for the prize. Such a person goes into great detail about what he has seen, and his unspiritual mind puffs him up with idle notions (2:18).

Here, Paul is talking about a spiritual deception that is as real and perilous today as it was in the first century A.D. It is the belief that if we can contact invisible spirits or the dead and get messages from them, we can access hidden spiritual power and knowledge. The Colossian Christians were troubled with these influences, just as we are. Today, we see a growing influence of the New Age, occultism, astrology, satanism, magic, seances, and more. All of these practices are deceptive, satanic substitutes for the indwelling power of Jesus Christ.

Then, in chapter 3, the apostle turns to the *true manifestation of power* and how to lay hold of the power of Christ:

Since, then, you have been raised with Christ, set your hearts on things above, where Christ is seated at the right hand of God. Set your minds on things above, not on earthly things (vv. 1–2).

Paul is not saying that we should go around constantly thinking about heaven. He is simply saying, "Don't let your desires and your attitudes be governed or directed by desires for earthly fame or power. Instead, let your desires be shaped by the Word of God." We are to exhibit love, truth, faith, and patience—the qualities that mark the life of the risen Lord. We are to manifest heaven in our everyday situations. And Paul gives us the recipe for carrying out this mission:

> **Let your desires and attitudes be shaped by the Word of God.**

Put to death, therefore, whatever belongs to your earthly nature: sexual immorality, impurity, lust, evil desires and greed, which is idolatry (3:5).

God has already sentenced the earthly nature to death on the cross. When it manifests itself in us, we must treat it like a guilty prisoner under sentence of death from God. We are not to compromise with any of these practices. We are to put them away. That is step number one. Step two is found in verses 12 through 14:

> *As God's chosen people, holy and dearly loved, clothe yourselves with*
> *compassion, kindness, humility, gentleness and patience. Bear with*
> *each other and forgive whatever grievances you may have against*
> *one another. Forgive as the Lord forgave you. And over all these*
> *virtues put on love, which binds them all together in perfect unity.*

What does Paul mean by this? He is telling us that Christ already dwells in us. Since He lives within us, the challenge to us is simply to get ourselves out of His way and allow His life to be manifest in us. We are to allow these Christlike characteristics to bubble forth in our lives. His life in us will make them authentic not artificial.

Paul goes on to list certain areas in which these characteristics are to show forth in us:

> *Wives, submit to your husbands, as is fitting in the Lord.*
> *Husbands, love your wives and do not be harsh with them.*
> *Children, obey your parents in everything, for this pleases the Lord.*
> *Fathers, do not embitter your children, or they will become*
> *discouraged.*
> *Slaves, obey your earthly masters in everything; and do it, not only*
> *when their eye is on you and to win their favor, but with sincerity of*
> *heart and reverence for the Lord. . . .*
> *Masters, provide your slaves with what is right and fair, because*
> *you know that you also have a Master in heaven (3:18–22; 4:1).*

All of our relationships, from family relationships to our relationships with those under our authority and over us in authority, must exhibit the character and love of Jesus Christ. His life is to shine through our lives.

The Basis for Joy

Paul concludes his letter to the Colossians with these practical admonitions:

> *Devote yourselves to prayer, being watchful and thankful. And pray*
> *for us, too, that God may open a door for our message, so that we*
> *may proclaim the mystery of Christ, for which I am in chains. Pray*
> *that I may proclaim it clearly, as I should. Be wise in the way you*
> *act toward outsiders; make the most of every opportunity (4:2–5).*

Then he continues with personal greetings from those who are with him. He concludes the letter, as was his custom, by taking the pen in his own hand and writing:

> I, Paul, write this greeting in my own hand. Remember my chains. Grace be with you (4:18).

The Key to Colossians

I said at the beginning of this chapter that Paul expresses the theme of Colossians in his introductory prayer (1:10–12), and this is where we find the key to the entire book:

> We pray this [for knowledge of God's will, for wisdom, for understanding] in order that you may live a life worthy of the Lord . . . being strengthened with all power according to his glorious might (1:10–11).

What a tremendous truth! Don't we all want that? Don't we, as Christians, want to see Christ's power, Christ's life, manifested in us? Not so that we can dazzle people, but so that we can experience everything that God intended for us: "joyfully giving thanks to the Father, who has qualified you to share in the inheritance of the saints in the kingdom of light" (1:11–12). And what He intends for us to experience is nothing less than joy!

The world cannot produce joyful living. The world can give us excitement, thrills, highs—a whole range of intense, fleeting emotions—but the world cannot give us genuine joy. The world cannot help us endure trials with courage or accept hardships with faith and patience. This takes the kind of power found only in Jesus Christ—a power that can transform our hardships and our difficulties into joyful experiences, not just phony, superficial manifestations of feel-good happiness. True joy enables us to learn and grow through trials.

If our hearts are right with Christ, if we are putting off the old and putting on the new, then we can go through tough times—experiences that would produce grumbling, griping, and despair in others—and we can find joy! Genuine, lasting, dependable, reliable, supernatural joy! That is what Paul means when he writes, "Christ in you, the hope of glory." That is the message of Colossians.

> Christ in you—
> the hope of glory.

NOTES

NOTES

ADVENTURING
through
PAUL'S EPISTLES

CHAPTER NINE

1 THESSALONIANS: HOPE *for a* HOPELESS WORLD

SOME YEARS AGO, A TEAM of archaeologists was digging in an ancient part of the Greek city of Thessaloniki—also called Salonika or Thessalonica—a port city in Macedonia, northeastern Greece. As they excavated, the archaeologists uncovered a Grecian cemetery dating back to the first century A.D. Among the pagan tombstones, they found one that was inscribed in Greek with these words: "No Hope." How ironic, then, that as we examine Paul's first letter to the Christians who lived in that same city during that same era we find that his theme is the hope of the believer!

As we adventure through the book of 1 Thessalonians, we will see that the Christians to whom Paul wrote this letter lived during a time of great upheaval, persecution, and peril. The world around them was coming apart at the seams. Yet Paul's message to them was, "Take heart! Have hope! Jesus is returning, God is in control, and He knows what He is doing!"

The Background of 1 Thessalonians

Many of the cities where Paul preached and founded churches have long since crumbled into ruin, but Thessaloniki is still a thriving, bustling metropolis. A Roman province in Paul's day, the city of Thessaloniki or Thessalonica has had a troubled history. It was occupied by the Saracens in the tenth century, by the Normans in the twelfth, by the Turks from 1430 to 1912, and by the Nazis in World War II.

> Paul's founding of the church at Thessalonica is recorded in Acts 17.

The account of Paul's founding of the church at Thessalonica is recorded in Acts 17. After Paul and Silas were thrown into prison in Philippi for preaching the gospel, an earthquake shook the prison, breaking the prison doors and freeing the prisoners. Fortunately for the Philippian jailer, who would have been executed if any prisoners escaped, none of the prisoners fled. Paul was then officially set free by the Roman magistrates, and he left Philippi and went to Thessalonica.

From the account in Acts we learn that Paul was there for only about three weeks when persecution arose, forcing him to leave the city for his own safety. He went down to Athens and from there he sent Timothy back to see how the Christians were doing. He was very concerned about them, fearful that the persecution they were undergoing would harm their newborn faith.

Paul then went on to Corinth, where he founded another church after several months of difficult labor. Later, Timothy returned to him at Corinth, bringing word of how the Thessalonians were doing and of some of the problems they were facing.

Paul's first letter to the Thessalonians was written about A.D. 50, making it the first of Paul's epistles. In fact, it may well be the first written book of the New Testament, although some Bible scholars believe the gospels of Matthew and (perhaps) Mark can be dated as early as A.D. 43 to 45. This letter was written to a struggling yet vigorous church that was only a few months old and was made up of Christians who had just come to Christ under Paul's ministry. It is a delightfully personal letter, revealing the heart of the apostle toward these new Christians and showing the intense struggles that the early Christians were undergoing in that city.

The Structure and Outline of 1 Thessalonians

The first letter to the Thessalonians can be divided into two major sections. In the first three chapters, the apostle pours out his heart concerning his relationship to them. In the final two chapters, Paul gives them practical instruction in how to live and experience the believer's hope amid the pressures of life.

Paul's Personal Relationship with the Thessalonian Christians (1 Thessalonians 1–3)

1.	Paul affirms the Thessalonians for their growth	1
2.	How Paul founded the Thessalonian church	2:1–16
3.	How Timothy strengthened the church	2:17–3:10
4.	Paul's desire to visit the Thessalonians	3:11–13

Paul Gives the Thessalonians Practical Instruction—and Eternal Hope (1 Thessalonians 4–5)

5.	Instructions for growth	4:1–12
6.	The dead in Christ will be raised	4:13–18
7.	The coming Day of the Lord	5:1–11
8.	Instructions for righteous living	5:12–22
9.	Conclusion	5:23–28

Familiar-Sounding Problems

Today, we live in a world that is increasingly hostile toward Christianity. In many countries, Christians are persecuted or killed for their faith. In fact, it is not difficult to imagine that even in America, Christians soon may be actively persecuted for their faith by the increasingly godless society around us, and even by the government.

That was the kind of environment surrounding Paul and the Thessalonian Christians. Wherever the apostle Paul went, he was hounded by a group of Jews who told others that he was not a genuine apostle because he was not one of the original twelve. And the Thessalonian Christians were severely persecuted by the pagans of Thessalonica, who threatened them, abused them, and seized their property. Here were new Christians—some were only days or weeks old in the faith—being called upon to endure extreme hardship for their newfound Lord.

> **New Christians were being called upon to endure extreme hardship for their newfound Lord.**

Also, just as we live today in an age of heightened sexual permissiveness and promiscuity, so did the people of first-century Greek society. Their religion sanctioned sexual promiscuity. The priestesses of the pagan temples were often prostitutes, practicing their trade in the temples. And those who practiced moral purity were regarded as laughable freaks.

Confusion over the Second Coming

Another major problem in this church was confusion over the second coming of Jesus Christ. The apostle had evidently told them about the Lord's eventual return, but they had misunderstood part of his teaching. Some expected Christ to come back so soon that they had actually stopped working for a living; they were simply waiting for Him to come and take them away. Since they weren't earning a living, somebody had to take care of them, and they had become leeches on the rest of the congregation. Also, there were developing tensions between the congregation and church leaders. Finally, some of them were somewhat indifferent to the Holy Spirit's work among them, and to the truth of God proclaimed in the Scriptures.

Do those problems sound familiar? We can't deny our likeness to the Thessalonian church.

Three Qualities of the Thessalonians

In the first section of the letter, chapters 1 through 3, Paul pours his heart out for these early Christians. He is afraid that they might have misunderstood his leaving Thessalonica, perhaps thinking he had abandoned them to avoid persecution. So he reminds them that he has just come through a terrible time of persecution in Philippi and that his own heart is deeply concerned for them. The key to Paul's heart is found at the beginning of this section:

We always thank God for all of you, mentioning you in our prayers. We continually remember before our God and Father your work produced by faith, your labor prompted by love, and your endurance inspired by hope in our Lord Jesus Christ (1:2–3).

Three qualities marked the Thessalonian believers: their work of faith, their labor of love, and their endurance in hope. These are detailed more clearly later in this chapter where we read:

They tell how you turned to God from idols [that was the Thessalonians' work of faith] to serve the living and true God [that was their labor of love], and to wait for his Son from heaven, whom he raised from the dead—Jesus [that is their patience, evidenced by their waiting in hope for His Son from heaven], who rescues us from the coming wrath (1:9–10).

Interestingly enough, those three qualities of the Thessalonians serve as a brief outline, built right into the text, to guide our understanding of the first three chapters of the book: the work of faith (chapter 1), the labor of love (chapter 2), and the patience of hope (chapter 3).

In chapter 1, Paul reminds them that the words he spoke to them when he founded the Thessalonian church were not merely the words of a human being:

The Work of Faith

Our gospel came to you not simply with words, but also with power, with the Holy Spirit and with deep conviction. You know how we lived among you for your sake (1:5).

The gospel Paul preached came not only in word but also in power and in the Holy Spirit. When the Thessalonians believed in his words and turned from their former devotion to idols, they performed the work of faith. Suddenly, these people who once lived in a condition of powerlessness had power. These people who once lived in a condition of hopelessness had hope. They had a reason for living, they had purpose, and they had the Holy Spirit living out His life through them.

In chapter 2, Paul gives us a wonderful description of the labor of love. This is not only the labor of the Thessalonians, but Paul's labor as well. In verses 9 through 12, we find this powerful description:

The Labor of Love

> *Surely you remember, brothers, our toil and hardship; we worked*
> *night and day in order not to be a burden to anyone while we*
> *preached the gospel of God to you.*
> *You are witnesses, and so is God, of how holy, righteous and*
> *blameless we were among you who believed. For you know that*
> *we dealt with each of you as a father deals with his own children,*
> *encouraging, comforting and urging you to live lives worthy of*
> *God, who calls you into his kingdom and glory (2:9–12).*

This was Paul's labor of love. And the Thessalonians evidently did what Paul exhorted them to do, for he goes on to say:

> *You, brothers, became imitators of God's churches in Judea, which*
> *are in Christ Jesus (2:14).*

This is the service, the labor of love of the Thessalonians.

The Patience of Hope Chapter 3 is an account of how Paul sent Timothy to the Thessalonians, and how Timothy brought back word of the persecution they were undergoing—and especially of their patience and endurance amid the persecution. This is a powerful description of the patience of hope, which enabled the Thessalonian Christians to endure trials with joy.

Practical Advice on How to Live

Chapters 4 and 5, the practical section of this letter, are divided into four brief sections that address the problems this church confronted. The apostle's first exhortation is to live cleanly in the midst of a sex-saturated society, and he begins by reminding them that he has already taught them how to live:

> *Brothers, we instructed you how to live in order to please God, as*
> *in fact you are living. Now we ask you and urge you in the Lord*
> *Jesus to do this more and more (4:1).*

He had not taught them, as many people think Christianity teaches, that they ought to live a good, clean life. Buddhism teaches that. Islam teaches that. Most religions advocate a moral lifestyle—and Christianity certainly does, but that's not its sole emphasis. Christianity is not so much concerned with rules and laws but with a relationship. Because we have a living, love relationship with God through Jesus Christ, we want to please God.

Now, what one quality of life is essential to pleasing God? Faith! Without faith it is impossible to please God. You cannot please Him by your own efforts, struggling to live up to a self-imposed standard or one that someone else has imposed upon you. You please Him by depending on Him alone and, by faith, allowing Him to live His life through you. And this kind of life produces behavior that is morally pure.

> **Because we have a living, love relationship with God through Jesus Christ, we want to please God.**

This is not to say that we will be perfect, but we will be making progress, and perfection in Christ (not our own strength) will be our continuous goal. If Christians are characterized by impurity, that is a clear sign that we are not living a life of faith. As Paul says,

> *It is God's will that you should be sanctified: that you should avoid sexual immorality; that each of you should learn to control his own body in a way that is holy and honorable, not in passionate lust like the heathen, who do not know God; and that in this matter no one should wrong his brother or take advantage of him. The Lord will punish men for all such sins, as we have already told you and warned you. For God did not call us to be impure, but to live a holy life. Therefore, he who rejects this instruction does not reject man but God, who gives you his Holy Spirit (4:3–8).*

This is what God expects of those who are in a living, faith relationship with Him.

The second problem Paul takes up is the matter of living honestly and productively. As he says in 1 Thessalonians 4:9–12, we are to show love toward one another, and the practical manifestation of that love is for all to get busy and work with their hands so they won't have to depend upon somebody else for support. God does not want us to enable laziness or subsidize unproductive people. Rather, Paul tells each person

> *to mind your own business and to work with your hands, just as we told you, so that your daily life may win the respect of outsiders and so that you will not be dependent on anybody (4:11–12).*

Our Present and Future Hope

In verse 13, we come to the major problem in the Thessalonian church, as well as the crowning theme of this book: the Thessalonians' misunderstanding about the coming of the Lord and their reason to hope. The Thessalonian Christians had gotten the idea that when Jesus Christ returned to earth the second time to begin His millennial kingdom, those who were alive would enter with Him into this kingdom, and they were expecting the Lord's return within their lifetime. But what about those who had died in the meantime? Wouldn't they miss out on all the benefits and the blessings of the Millennium?

> **"The major problem in the Thessalonian church was the Thessalonians' misunderstanding about the coming of the Lord and their reason to hope."**

This thinking probably arose because of a misunderstanding of the doctrine of resurrection. They were thinking in terms of one resurrection, a single event that would occur at the end of the Millennium, when the dead would be raised, good and evil alike, to stand before the judgment seat of God. And there are passages, of course, that do speak of a resurrection to come at the end of the Millennium. Paul points out, however, that the resurrection does not proceed as a single event but that groups of believers are resurrected at various times. Notice his argument:

> *Brothers, we do not want you to be ignorant about those who fall asleep, or to grieve like the rest of men, who have no hope. We believe that Jesus died and rose again and so we believe that God will bring with Jesus those who have fallen asleep in him (4:13–14).*

In other words, those who have died are going to be raised again; and they'll come back with Jesus when He comes to establish His millennial reign. But this presents another problem: How will they come back with Jesus in bodily form when their bodies have been placed in the grave? What reassurance can believers have that this claim is true? "Ah," says the apostle Paul, "let me give you a revelation I received from the Lord!"

> *According to the Lord's own word, we tell you that we who are still alive, who are left till the coming of the Lord, will certainly not precede those who have fallen asleep. For the Lord himself will come down from heaven, with a loud command, with the voice of the archangel and with the trumpet call of God, and the dead in Christ will rise first. After that, we who are still alive and are left will be caught up together with them in the clouds to meet the*

Lord in the air. And so we will be with the Lord forever. Therefore encourage each other with these words (4:15–18).

Paul is describing an aspect of the Lord's coming that takes place before His return to establish the millennial-kingdom reign. He is coming for His people, to gather those who are His to be with Him, in His presence, before His return to establish the kingdom. This first return is called the *Parousia* in Greek and does not refer to the second coming of Christ. At this first return, this *Parousia*, the dead in Christ will be raised, so that we all will be with Him when He is ready to establish His kingdom. So you see how this doctrine answers their problem? The Thessalonians who have lost loved ones need not grieve over those who have died, because those who have died in Christ will actually precede those who are alive when the Lord comes for His own.

The Parousia

By comparing this passage with other passages of the Old and New Testaments, we know that between that *Parousia* and the Lord's coming to establish the kingdom will come a seven-year period of great worldwide tribulation. Paul goes on to speak of this period in chapter 5:

The Tribulation

Brothers, about times and dates we do not need to write to you, for you know very well that the day of the Lord will come like a thief in the night (5:1–2).

Nobody can set a date for this event. It will come suddenly, quickly. And when the Lord comes in the *Parousia*, two great chains of events will be set in motion. The Lord will begin one series of events in which all believers will be caught up to be with Him, and at the same time, He will begin another series of events on earth known as the Great Tribulation—or, as it is called in the Old Testament, the Day of the Lord.

There are two "days" that we need to distinguish in Scripture: the Day of the Lord and the Day of Christ. They both begin at exactly the same time, but they concern two distinct bodies of people. The Day of Christ concerns believers, while the Day of the Lord refers to what is happening to unbelievers during this time.

The Day of the Lord and the Day of Christ

It is my personal conviction, from my study of Scripture, that when the Lord comes for His own, when the dead in Christ rise, and when we who are alive are caught up with them to be with the Lord, we don't leave this planet! We stay here with the Lord, visibly directing the events of the tribulation period as they break out in great judgmental sequences upon the ones who are living as mortals upon the earth. The terrible scenes of that day are vividly portrayed in the book of Revelation.

The apostle Paul says to the Thessalonian believers that no one knows when this is going to happen:

> *While people are saying, "Peace and safety," destruction will come on them suddenly, as labor pains on a pregnant woman, and they will not escape.*
> *But you, brothers, are not in darkness so that this day should surprise you like a thief (5:3–4).*

This day will surprise the people of the world like a thief—but it needn't surprise you like a thief, because you are looking forward to it!

Paul tells us that we should not "go to sleep" as others of this world do; we should stay awake, sober, and on alert. We should never assume that life is simply going on as usual. We must be aware of what God is doing throughout history and eternity, and we must act accordingly. These signs are given us in Scripture so that we can be spiritually prepared and not caught unaware, as Paul tells us:

> *Let us not be like others, who are asleep, but let us be alert and self-controlled. For those who sleep, sleep at night, and those who get drunk, get drunk at night. But since we belong to the day, let us be self-controlled, putting on faith and love as a breastplate, and the hope of salvation as a helmet (5:6–8).*

Paul is not talking here about salvation from hell. He is referring to the salvation to come—that is, salvation from the wrath of God during the time of the judgment. He goes on to add,

> *God did not appoint us to suffer wrath but to receive salvation through our Lord Jesus Christ. He died for us so that, whether we are awake or asleep, we may live together with him. Therefore encourage one another and build each other up, just as in fact you are doing (5:9–11).*

Here was the complete answer to the Thessalonians' distress. They did not need to be discouraged or frightened. Rather, they could go on about their lives, confident that God was in charge of all matters pertaining to life, death, and beyond. And although times were extremely perilous, they could busy themselves with the work of the Lord, knowing that they were investing themselves in a certain future.

Living in Peace

The concluding section of this letter speaks not only of living confidently, but of living peacefully in the midst of troubled and uncertain conditions:

> We ask you, brothers, to respect those who work hard among you, who are over you in the Lord and who admonish you. Hold them in the highest regard in love because of their work. Live in peace with each other (5:12–13).

Animosity was developing toward some of the church leaders, and Paul says, "Remember that these people are concerned about your souls' welfare, and although they may have to speak rather sharply at times, it's not because they want to hurt you, but to help you. Therefore, remember that and live at peace with them and with each other. Love your leaders, because they serve you."

He follows this with admonitions against idleness, encouragement for the fainthearted, help for the needy, and patience for all. Then comes the most important admonition of all:

> Make sure that nobody pays back wrong for wrong, but always try to be kind to each other and to everyone else (5:15).

Without a doubt, this is one of the most frequently broken commands in Scripture. A famous bumper sticker says, "Don't get mad, get even!" But most of us, when someone offends, usually do both! We get mad—and we get even. This is tragically true even in the church. But this is worldly thinking. It has nothing to do with the grace, truth, and love of Jesus Christ. Above every other virtue, the virtue of forgiveness characterizes the gospel.

Paul then goes on to tell the Thessalonian believers to rejoice, pray continually, and give thanks. After various other admonitions, his final prayer for them—and for all believers who read this powerful letter, including you and me—is a beautiful prayer:

> Rejoice, pray continually, and give thanks.

May God himself, the God of peace, sanctify you through and through. May your whole spirit, soul and body be kept blameless at the coming of our Lord Jesus Christ (5:23).

Those words sum up the great overarching theme of 1 Thessalonians, for they sum up the hope of all believers: One day we shall all stand before God, and the whole spirit, soul, and body shall be blameless in that day, thanks to what Jesus Christ has done for us. What a blessing! What a hope!

NOTES

NOTES

NOTES

ADVENTURING *through* PAUL'S EPISTLES

CHAPTER TEN

2 THESSALONIANS: HOLDING BACK LAWLESSNESS

BEFORE JESUS CHRIST LEFT THIS EARTH, He said that He would return—but before His return, there would be a time of trial, persecution, and widespread lawlessness. The seams of society would be ripped apart, and violence would become so widespread that people's hearts would literally fail them for fear of coming events. It would be a time of global tribulation, said Jesus, "unequaled from the beginning of the world until now—and never to be equaled again" (Matt. 24:21).

Paul Corrects Misunder-standings As the Christians of Thessalonica were going through their time of trial, many thought they were experiencing that foretold time of tribulation. The apostle Paul wrote this second letter to correct certain misunderstandings they had about the Day of the Lord, a time of unequaled trouble and tribulation for the world.

The Outline of 2 Thessalonians

This letter has only three chapters, and each one is a correction of a common attitude that many people, even today, have about troubled times.

Paul's Encouragement for a Time of Trial (2 Thessalonians 1)

1. Paul's thankfulness for the Thessalonians	1:1–4
2. Encouragement for trials and persecution	1:5–10
3. Paul's prayer for God's blessing	1:11–12

The Day of the Lord (2 Thessalonians 2)

4. Signs of the approaching Day of the Lord	2:1–7
5. The second coming of Christ	2:8–12
6. The Christian's hope in the Day of the Lord	2:13–17

The Conduct of Believers under Pressure (2 Thessalonians 3)

7. Patience; avoid the disorderly	3:1–15
8. Conclusion	3:16–18

Encouragement for Trials and Persecution

The first chapter of this letter is devoted to the attitude of discouragement in times of trial. These Christians were undergoing persecutions and afflictions, and though they were bearing up remarkably well, many were becoming weary and discouraged. "Why try any more?" they groaned. "There's no justice. Everything is always against us."

To counteract this attitude, Paul reminds them that a day is coming when God will set everything right and repay them for their sufferings.

In 1 Thessalonians 1:4–10, Paul writes:

> *We know, brothers loved by God, that he has chosen you, because our gospel came to you not simply with words, but also with power, with the Holy Spirit and with deep conviction. You know how we lived among you for your sake. You became imitators of us and of the Lord; in spite of severe suffering, you welcomed the message with the joy given by the Holy Spirit. And so you became a model to all the believers in Macedonia and Achaia. The Lord's message rang out from you not only in Macedonia and Achaia—your faith in God has become known everywhere. Therefore we do not need to say anything about it, for they themselves report what kind of reception you gave us. They tell how you turned to God from idols to serve the living and true God, and to wait for his Son from heaven, whom he raised from the dead—Jesus, who rescues us from the coming wrath.*

We in America have not undergone much persecution during the two-hundred-plus years of our history, although today we see indications that a time of persecution may be looming. Our culture, media, courts, and government increasingly challenge our religious liberty, as well as our Christian faith and morality. In many parts of the world, however, Christians suffer and die for their faith, and the day may come when we, too, will have to choose between standing for our faith and life itself. If that day comes, we will fully appreciate the meaning of Paul's words in this letter.

> The day may come when we, too, will have to choose between standing for our faith and life itself.

Paul reminds the Thessalonians that God has not forgotten them and that ultimately His will and judgment will prevail.

When people go through a time of great persecution, they say, "Isn't there going to be a time when this injustice is corrected? How can a man like Hitler get away with killing so many Jews? How can a man like Stalin get away with killing so many of his own people? Why do corrupt dictators and leaders stay in power? Why doesn't God punish these horrible evil-doers now? Why does He wait so long to straighten things out?"

But Paul says, "Have faith! Be patient!" A day is coming when a three-fold repayment will be made. *First,* believers will be repaid for their sufferings, because these trials build their endurance and make them worthy of the coming kingdom of God. *Second,* the unbelieving will be repaid for

A Threefold Repayment

their unbelief and the misused opportunities in life; they will face the righteous Judge who knows their hearts, and He will exclude them from His presence. *Third*, the Lord Himself will be repaid, for He will "be glorified in his holy people and . . . marveled at among all those who have believed" (2 Thess. 1:10).

Notice, Paul does not say that God will be glorified *by* His people, but *in* His people when He takes sinful, fearful, powerless, self-centered human beings and infuses His character qualities, His love and joy, into their lives for the entire world to see. It is not a question of praise being offered to God from our lips but of God's receiving glory in the world as His personality is lived out through the quiet example of our lives. That is one of the most powerful ways in which God is glorified.

Now, let's take a closer look at the payment the unbelieving will receive. That payment is what the Bible calls "hell."

Hell is widely thought of as a fiery furnace where people in chains experience the torment of being continually, unrelentingly burned with fire. The Bible does use symbols of hell that support this idea, but I believe that the most literal understanding we can have of hell is that it is a condition of being forever excluded from the Lord's presence. God is the source of everything good: beauty, truth, life, love, joy, peace, grace, strength, forgiveness. All those things come only from God, and if someone chooses sin and self-will over these good things, God finally says to that person, "I've been trying to give you My best, but you prefer the worst. Have it your own way." When that person gets what he or she has demanded throughout life, it will be the last thing that person wants.

> The most literal understanding of hell is that it is a condition of being forever excluded from the Lord's presence.

The Day of the Lord Explained

Paul opens the second chapter of 2 Thessalonians by addressing the fears of the Thessalonian Christians. In verses 1 and 2, we read:

> *Concerning the coming of our Lord Jesus Christ and our being gathered to him, we ask you, brothers, not to become easily unsettled or alarmed by some prophecy, report or letter supposed to have come from us, saying that the day of the Lord has already come.*

The Thessalonians, who were already undergoing a time of terrible persecution, had evidently received a letter from somebody signing Paul's name, telling them that the day of the Lord had come and that times were going from bad to worse. Their minds were becoming unsettled by all that was happening around them. So Paul tells them, in effect, "Don't be shaken out of your wits by what is happening or by people who are trying to get you rattled."

Paul reminds them that he has already explained the difference between the Day of the Lord and the time of the Lord's coming to gather His people to be with Him. When the Lord comes for His people, He will descend from heaven with a shout and the voice of the archangel and the trumpet of God. The dead in Christ will be raised, and we who remain will be caught up together with them in the clouds to meet the Lord in the air. That is our gathering together to Jesus.

But the Day of the Lord, the terrible time of judgment, is a different event altogether. Having introduced the subject of the Day of the Lord, Paul goes on to tell them what it will be like and how they can tell it's coming:

The Day of
the Lord

> *Don't let anyone deceive you in any way, for that day will not come until the rebellion [or departure] occurs and the man of lawlessness is revealed, the man doomed to destruction. He will oppose and will exalt himself over everything that is called God or is worshiped, so that he sets himself up in God's temple, proclaiming himself to be God (2:3–4).*

I believe the word *rebellion* used in this translation is misleading. Literally translated, the original Greek word means "a departure." Many translators have taken this to suggest a departure from faith—that is, rebellion. I don't agree. I believe this departure refers to the departure of the church when Jesus comes to gather His people to Himself.

I find this to be an amazing passage, especially when we link it with the rest of Scripture, such as the Gospels. When Jesus was here, He offered Himself to the Jewish people as the promised Messiah, and most of them rejected Him. That is what John says in the opening verses of his gospel: "He came to that which was his own, but his own did not receive him" (John 1:11). That is what Jesus said to the people: "I have come in my Father's name, and you do not accept me; but if someone else comes in his own name, you will accept him" (John 5:43). Who is this person Jesus is talking about, this "someone else" who would come in his own name and be accepted where Jesus Himself was rejected? It is the same person Paul talks about, the one he calls "the man of lawlessness . . . , the man doomed to destruction."

Who is this man of lawlessness? Well, Paul tells us that he will be an utterly godless individual, yet so remarkable that people will actually accept him as a divinely empowered being who could deliver them from their difficulties. He will have extraordinary powers of communication and persuasion, and people will see him and believe that evil is good. The world is hungry to follow such a leader. Even today's diplomats, politicians, and leaders are looking for a single leader of leaders who can unite the world and bring us into harmony and peace. This man of lawlessness will be revealed in the temple of God in Jerusalem, says Paul.

When Paul wrote this letter in about A.D. 52, the temple in Jerusalem was still standing, but in A.D. 70 it was destroyed, and it has never been rebuilt. In fact, a great Islamic mosque, the Dome of the Rock, now squats on the site where the temple used to be. Scripture predicts that, somehow, the Jews will find a way to reconstruct another temple on the site in Jerusalem where the Dome of the Rock is now. And it is in that future temple, says Paul, that the man of lawlessness will take his seat. In 2 Thessalonians 2:5–8, Paul goes on to say:

> Don't you remember that when I was with you I used to tell you these things? And now you know what is holding him back, so that he may be revealed at the proper time. For the secret power of lawlessness is already at work; but the one who now holds it back will continue to do so till he is taken out of the way. And then the lawless one will be revealed, whom the Lord Jesus will overthrow with the breath of his mouth and destroy by the splendor of his coming.

This mystery, "the secret power of lawlessness," has baffled our world's leaders and thinkers throughout the centuries. As Philippine ambassador to the United States Carlos Romulo once said, "We have harnessed the power of the atom, but how can we bridle the passions of men?" The spirit of lawlessness, of sinfulness, of self-willed rebellion against authority and lust for power poses the greatest danger to any nation. Indeed, in this age of weapons of mass destruction, it is a threat to the existence of the entire human race.

But Paul says that something is restraining the power of lawlessness, preventing total anarchy. Jesus made it clear what that restraining force is: "You are the salt of the earth," He said. "You are the light of the world" (Matt.

5:13–14). Salt prevents corruption from spreading. Light dispels darkness. So it is the presence of God's people on earth that restrains the secret power of lawlessness and evil. But before we become proud, we should understand this: It is not we who hold back the darkness, but the Spirit of God, living in us, acting through us. So we must make sure that the Holy Spirit has all there is of us so that He can be fully present in the world, guarding against corruption, illuminating the dark corners of this world.

"The secret power of lawlessness is already at work," says Paul, "but the one who now holds it back [the Holy Spirit] will continue to do so till he is taken out of the way." The restraint that holds back the darkness is going to be removed, and then the whole flood of human evil will be let loose upon the earth. When Jesus comes to gather His people out of the world, the Holy Spirit—who lives in all of us who follow Jesus Christ—will be removed from the world. The restraining force will be gone. Lawlessness will reign on earth, but only for a brief period of time. At the end of that period, the man of lawlessness, who is also called the Antichrist, will be defeated and the worldwide reign of evil will come to an end. As Paul writes:

The Power of Lawlessness Released

> *The lawless one will be revealed, whom the Lord Jesus will overthrow with the breath of his mouth and destroy by the splendor of his coming. The coming of the lawless one will be in accordance with the work of Satan displayed in all kinds of counterfeit miracles, signs and wonders, and in every sort of evil that deceives those who are perishing. They perish because they refused to love the truth and so be saved. For this reason God sends them a powerful delusion so that they will believe the lie and so that all will be condemned who have not believed the truth but have delighted in wickedness (2:8–12).*

God has planted truth inside every human being, yet some choose to believe the lie. So God gives them over to a powerful delusion, and those who willfully delight in wickedness remain mired in the lie until their self-deception and self-destruction is complete. The lie, and all those who believe it, will be destroyed by the coming of Jesus, the Son of Man, who will destroy the destroyer.

The Conduct of Believers Under Pressure

Chapter 3 deals with the conduct of believers in the face of difficulty and pressure.

Certain people in Thessalonica were saying, "Why not just wait until

Jesus comes back for us? Why should we concern ourselves about making a living? Let's just live and enjoy ourselves and wait for His coming." So Paul says to them:

> *In the name of the Lord Jesus Christ, we command you, brothers, to keep away from every brother who is idle and does not live according to the teaching you received from us (v. 6).*

Paul's statement is occasioned by facts that he describes in verses 11 through 13:

> *We hear that some among you are idle. They are not busy; they are busybodies. Such people we command and urge in the Lord Jesus Christ to settle down and earn the bread they eat. And as for you, brothers, never tire of doing what is right.*

As we get nearer to the time of His coming, Paul says, remember that your responsibility is to keep on living normally and working with your hands, taking care of your responsibilities. The Christian life is a normal, natural life, which involves fulfilling all the responsibilities that God places upon us. So, Paul rejects the irrational fanaticism that says, "Let's just drop everything and wait for Jesus to take us away." That is not reasonable, realistic, or even spiritual. It is just lazy and foolish. No one knows when Jesus is coming for us. Although many signs seem to indicate that His return is imminent, He may not come for another thousand or ten thousand years. Only God the Father knows the day and the hour of the Lord's return.

Only God the Father knows the day and the hour of the Lord's return.

Many of the Thessalonian believers had been fooled once before by a forged letter purporting to be from Paul. To make sure this can't happen again, he gives them a sample of his own handwriting:

> *I, Paul, write this greeting in my own hand, which is the distinguishing mark in all my letters. This is how I write.*
> *The grace of our Lord Jesus Christ be with you all (3:17–18).*

With these words, Paul closes a very practical, powerful, and timely letter—timely even in our own day and age. The practical application of this letter to each heart is this: God's people are called to be restrainers of lawlessness, but in order to do so, we must allow God to have complete reign in our lives. If we operate in even the smallest degree by lawlessness, how can we restrain the lawlessness of this world? The measure in which you have dealt with and vanquished the lawlessness of your own heart will determine how effectively God can use you to restrain the lawlessness of this world.

After all these years, the hope of the church has not grown dim. Jesus is coming again, and our task is to patiently work, watch, wait, and hope until we hear the shout of triumph and see Him coming for us in the clouds.

NOTES

NOTES

ADVENTURING
through
PAUL'S EPISTLES

---

CHAPTER ELEVEN

1 TIMOTHY:
HOW *to* BUILD
a CHURCH

WHAT HAPPENS WHEN CHRISTIANS gather together at church? Charles Swindoll answers that question in this passage from his book *Come Before Winter and Share My Hope*:

> *See you Sunday. That's when the Body and the Head meet to celebrate this mysterious union . . . when ordinary, garden-variety folks like us gather around the pre-eminent One. For worship. For encouragement. For instruction. For expression. For support. For the carrying out of a God-given role that will never be matched or surpassed on earth—even though it's the stuff the world around us considers weird and weak (Charles R. Swindoll,* Come Before Winter and Share My Hope *[Wheaton, Ill.: Tyndale, 1985], 403–4).*

Yes! Although the world truly does consider the church to be "weird and weak," we know that the church is the most powerful instrument in the world. Jesus Himself has said, "On this rock I will build my church, and the gates of Hades will not overcome it" (Matt. 16:18).

A Blueprint for Building the Church

In Paul's first letter to Timothy, we are given a set of detailed instructions, a blueprint that shows us how to build a church. Jesus Himself is the architect, the master builder, but we are the carpenters and bricklayers, painters, and carpet layers. So if we want to build His church in a way that pleases Him, we had better read the blueprint He has given us—the blueprint of 1 Timothy.

Paul's Letters to Timothy

Paul wrote two letters to Timothy. The second was unquestionably the last letter we have from his pen. The first was written a few years earlier, probably immediately after the apostle Paul was imprisoned in Rome for the first time. After he was released, he wrote this letter to the young man whom he had won to Christ when he preached in Timothy's hometown of Lystra.

Timothy was probably no more than sixteen years old at the time he found Christ, and he was probably in his late twenties or early thirties at the time this letter was written. He accompanied Paul on his second missionary journey and was a faithful minister and son in the faith to Paul for the rest of Paul's life.

> *This first letter to Timothy is one of three pastoral letters in the New Testament*

This first letter to Timothy is one of *three pastoral letters* in the New Testament—letters written from a pastor's viewpoint; the other two are

2 Timothy and Titus. In these letters, Paul expressed his intimate thoughts to the young people he was mentoring in the ministry, ones who frequently accompanied him on his journeys.

Despite his close teacher-mentor, father-son relationship with Timothy, Paul begins both of his letters with these similar, rather formal statements:

> *Paul, an apostle of Christ Jesus by the command of God our Savior and of Christ Jesus our hope (1 Tim. 1:1).*

> *Paul, an apostle of Christ Jesus by the will of God, according to the promise of life that is in Christ Jesus (2 Tim. 1:1).*

Timothy certainly did not need this reminder that Paul was an apostle of Christ Jesus; he knew Paul's position well. But Paul expected these letters to have a wider readership than Timothy alone. His previous letters had frequently been circulated among the churches, and he knew these letters would also be circulated. So it is with the authority of an apostle that Paul begins these two letters.

The apostles were men with a unique ministry. They had been commissioned by the Lord Himself and given the task of speaking authoritatively on doctrine and practice in the church. In the first century, some people spoke disparagingly of Paul, just as people sometimes do today. You've probably heard, just as I have: "Well, you know, Paul wrote some things that we cannot take as authoritative. He was a confirmed old bachelor, and what he said about women is not really significant." But to say such a thing is to deny the apostolic office and to refuse the authority that the Lord Jesus gave His apostles, including Paul.

The Authority of the Apostles

The Outline of 1 Timothy

Paul's first letter to Timothy concerns the ministry of the church itself: its character, its nature, and its function in the world. His second letter pertains to the message that the church is to convey to the world: the gospel of Jesus Christ and Timothy's relationship to that gospel. Here is a structural overview of 1 Timothy:

True and False Doctrines (1 Timothy 1)

1. The danger of false doctrine; teach the truth   1:1–17
2. Fight the good fight; hold onto faith   1:18–20

Church Worship (1 Timothy 2)

3. Rules for public worship; the role of women   2

Church Leadership (1 Timothy 3)

4. Qualifications of church leaders   3:1–13
    (bishops and deacons)
5. Conduct in God's household   3:14–16

Warnings against False Teachers (1 Timothy 4)

6. False and true teachers contrasted   4:1–10
7. Do not neglect the gift of God   4:11–16

Church Discipline (1 Timothy 5)

8. Treatment of all people   5:1–2
9. Treatment of widows   5:3–16
10. Treatment of elders   5:17–20
11. Avoid prejudice in church discipline   5:21–25

The Motives of a Church Leader (1 Timothy 6)

12. Exhortations to servants   6:1–2
13. Godliness with contentment is gain   6:3–16
14. Exhortation to the rich   6:17–19
15. Guard what has been entrusted to you   6:20–21

The True Christian Church and True Christian Love

Two themes intertwine throughout 1 Timothy: the true nature of the Christian church and the true nature of Christian love. A powerful expression of the first theme, the true nature of the church, is found in 1 Timothy 3:14–15:

> *Although I hope to come to you soon, I am writing you these instructions so that, if I am delayed, you will know how people ought to conduct themselves in God's household, which is the church of the living God, the pillar and foundation of the truth.*

When Paul writes about "the church of the living God," clearly he is not talking about a *building;* he is talking about *people.* In fact, he is talking about a family, God's household. One of the great weaknesses of present-day Christianity is that we tend to think of the church as a building. Paul wanted Timothy to know how to conduct himself in the ministry and in his relationships within the body of Christ, the church of the living God.

We find a powerful expression of the second theme of this letter, the true nature of Christian love, in 1 Timothy 1:5:

> *The goal of this command is love, which comes from a pure heart and a good conscience and a sincere faith.*

> **Paul wanted Timothy to know how to conduct himself in the ministry and in his relationships within the body of Christ.**

This is a more personal theme, concerned with the individual's relationship to the world, to other Christians, and to God. As the apostle puts it, this second theme states that the Christian's relationships are to consist of "love, which comes from a pure heart and a good conscience and a sincere faith."

Actually, we must always begin with the last of these qualities—a sincere faith—for that is how we came into the Christian life: by believing God's Word, by exercising faith in what He says. Then, we are led to a good conscience and a pure heart that loves in obedience to His Word. We all come to God in need of being purified by the washing of the Word of God and the cleansing of the blood of Christ. But if you have a good conscience about your faith, it will result in a pure heart, and from that pure heart will flow an unceasing stream of love.

The Danger of False Teaching

Timothy was pastoring the church in Ephesus, a city largely devoted to the worship of a pagan goddess, Diana (also called Artemis), the love goddess of the Greek world. Timothy's task was to minister to the church that was opposing the blind idolatry and superstition of this spiritually dark city, much as our task is to oppose the spiritual darkness and idolatry that surround us today. So the first counsel the apostle offers is that Timothy is to oppose false teaching.

The early church had its share of heretics, as does today's church, and apparently the Ephesian church was being infiltrated by false teachers. Paul warns Timothy:

> *As I urged you when I went into Macedonia, stay there in Ephesus so that you may command certain men not to teach false doctrines*

any longer nor to devote themselves to myths and endless genealogies. These promote controversies rather than God's work—which is by faith (1:3–4).

One of the problems in the church was a wrong understanding of the law. Some church leaders tried to control the conduct of the Ephesian Christians through regulations—in other words, legalism. These legalists who were infecting the church did not understand the power of the indwelling life and grace of the Lord Jesus Christ.

Using the law to control people, says Paul, is wrong. The law is intended for a specific and valid purpose, yet these legalists were abusing the law:

> **Legalists who were infecting the church did not understand the power of the indwelling life and grace of the Lord Jesus Christ.**

They want to be teachers of the law, but they do not know what they are talking about or what they so confidently affirm.

We know that the law is good if one uses it properly. We also know that law is made not for the righteous but for lawbreakers and rebels, the ungodly and sinful, the unholy and irreligious; for those who kill their fathers or mothers, for murderers, for adulterers and perverts, for slave traders and liars and perjurers—and for whatever else is contrary to the sound doctrine that conforms to the glorious gospel of the blessed God, which he entrusted to me (1:7–11).

The law, says Paul, is made for the unrighteous, not the righteous. If you have come to Christ, and your heart is intent upon pleasing Him, why do you need the law? You certainly don't need it to keep you from doing wrong. Love will take care of that! But remember that love is interpreted by the law. We understand what love is only when we see it spelled out for us in terms of the law: Do not lie, steal, kill, commit adultery and so forth. These laws describe how true love behaves.

Instructions for Public Worship

In chapter 2, Paul turns to instructions for public worship. He begins by differentiating between the roles of men and women in public worship. Men, he says, are to lead in prayer, praying for kings and those in authority, so that citizens might live in peace and godliness. Then he turns to the role of women in the church, and this passage is sometimes used (usually by men) to suggest that women have an inferior position in the church.

We must understand the significant difference between someone's *role* Roles of Men and Women in Public Worship and someone's *importance*. In the church we all have different roles, but we are all equally important. As Paul tells us in 1 Corinthians 12, the eye can't say to the hand, or the head to the feet, "I'm the important one here. The body does not need you as much as it needs me." All are necessary, all are equally important, but each has a different role to play. Paul differentiates between the roles of men and women in the church in these verses:

> *I want men everywhere to lift up holy hands in prayer, without anger or disputing.*
>
> *I also want women to dress modestly, with decency and propriety, not with braided hair or gold or pearls or expensive clothes, but with good deeds, appropriate for women who profess to worship God.*
>
> *A woman should learn in quietness and full submission. I do not permit a woman to teach or to have authority over a man; she must be silent. For Adam was formed first, then Eve. And Adam was not the one deceived; it was the woman who was deceived and became a sinner. But women will be saved through childbearing—if they continue in faith, love and holiness with propriety (1 Tim. 2:8–15).*

Paul is not saying that women have no right to minister and pray in public like men, although some have misunderstood this passage that way. Rather, he is saying that women are not to teach men authoritatively. They are not to be the final word in the church as to doctrine or teaching, and Paul gives two reasons. First, he says, Adam was formed first, then Eve. Second, the woman was deceived and therefore fell into transgression. It is interesting to note that Eve's sin was primarily that of trying to arrive at a theological conclusion apart from the counsel of her husband.

In a verse that has been somewhat garbled in translation and greatly misunderstood, the apostle goes on to show that women have a wonderful ministry. Women, he says, will be saved through bearing children, if they continue in faith and love and holiness, with modesty or propriety (v. 15). It is important to note, by the way, that the pronoun *they* refers to the children, not the women.

Now what does Paul mean when he says that women will be saved through bearing children? I have struggled long with this passage. Late in life, I have come to believe that we can understand the principle of this difficult passage through Paul's exhortation to Timothy in 1 Timothy 4:16:

Watch your life and doctrine closely. Persevere in them, because if you do, you will save both yourself and your hearers.

What does Paul mean by the word *save*? Timothy was already saved; he had been a Christian for many years. And certainly other people were not saved by Timothy's obeying the truth. What does he mean, then? Paul is using the word *salvation* in a different sense than we usually think of it. In fact, Paul uses the word *saved* or *salvation* similarly in several other letters. For example, in Philippians, Paul writes, "Work out your salvation with fear and trembling"—that is, work out the solutions to the problems you confront with fear and trembling, because "it is God who works in you to will and to act according to his good purpose" (Phil. 2:12–13). So here in 1 Timothy, I believe the meaning is that the woman "will be saved" in the sense that her desire for a ministry will be fulfilled and problems will be resolved through childbearing if the children continue in faith and love and holiness with modesty.

Church Leadership

Next, Paul turns to the qualifications of church leaders. These leaders fall into two major categories: bishops (or elders) and deacons. Broadly defined, bishops or elders are authorities or decision-makers in the church. Deacons are men and women who perform a special task or function in the church, such as caring for the sick and aged, working in an outreach ministry, or teaching a Sunday school class.

Elders and Deacons

Paul begins by stating *three crucial qualifications* for bishops or elders. *First,* they are to be "blameless," so as to avoid being disapproved. *Second,* they are to be pure; that is, they are to be people of proven integrity who understand how to tell the difference between good and evil and who live according to God's Word. Paul gives this requirement of purity so as to avoid pride. The great risk in placing a spiritually immature person in leadership is that he or she may be lifted up with pride and fall into the trap of the devil (pride is always a trap). *Third,* these people are to be of good repute, to avoid public scandal that would bring the whole ministry of the church into disgrace.

Deacons are treated similarly, but Paul adds one major instruction concerning deacons: they are first to be tested, to be given work to do on a trial basis. If they perform it well, they are recognized as people who can be trusted with responsibility in the work of the church. The importance of this charge is that it relates to the fact that the church is linked with the mystery of Christ. Christ is the greatest figure in the universe—everything relates to Him. Paul quotes a first-century hymn to set forth what he means:

> *Beyond all question, the mystery of godliness is great: He appeared in a body, was vindicated by the Spirit, was seen by angels, was preached among the nations, was believed on in the world, was taken up in glory (3:16).*

Paul puts the church in its proper perspective. We must select the leaders of the church carefully, because the church represents Jesus Christ to the world.

The Importance of Preaching the Truth

In chapter 4, Paul turns to the subject of apostasy. But before we discuss this, let's clarify our terms. Although the terms are often confused or used interchangeably by Christians today, an *apostate* is not the same as a *heretic*. A heretic is a misguided Christian, one who basically accepts and knows the Lord Jesus Christ, but who tends to go wrong in some particular doctrinal issue. But an apostate has never been a Christian, although an apostate testifies that he or she is a Christian. As John tells us in his first letter, "They went out from us, but they did not really belong to us. For if they had belonged to us, they would have remained with us; but their going showed that none of them belonged to us" (1 John 2:19).

In Matthew 13, the Lord tells the story of the sower who went out to sow the good seed of the kingdom. In the middle of the night, an enemy came in behind him, sowing weeds in the same fields. The good grain and the weeds came up together. Jesus said these good and bad plants would grow up together until the harvest, which is why we will never get rid of the apostates within the church. Apostate attitudes arise when people follow doctrines of demons, deceitful spirits. Apostasy is not rooted in twisted human ideas, but in the deliberately deceitful ideas of wicked spirits who sow spiritual "weed seed" in order to pollute the kingdom and lead people astray.

Apostates and Heretics

Paul goes on to say that only when the evil of the apostates becomes evident is Timothy to excommunicate them, not before. His first priority is not to weed out evil and deception but to preach the truth. His next priority is to set an example for the people in his own personal life.

> *Until I come, devote yourself to the public reading of Scripture, to preaching and to teaching. Do not neglect your gift, which was given you through a prophetic message when the body of elders laid their hands on you (4:13–14).*

Too many Christians have forgotten the message of Jesus and of Paul regarding apostasy. They see their ministry in the church as that of being a Christian weed-whacker, like one of those whirring garden implements that mows down weeds with nylon fishing line. Unfortunately, such Christians also whack down a lot of fruit-bearing plants as well! Both Jesus and Paul tell us not to go around whacking weeds but to keep the garden as strong and weed-resistant as it can possibly be. That means informing the congregation of the dangers, setting a positive example, and continually expounding the Scriptures.

Church Discipline and Other Admonitions

In chapter 5, Paul discusses specific issues and problems within the church, including how to treat younger and older people as well as advice to women on various practical matters. Then he takes up the official problem of how to handle accusations against the elders. Finally, he discusses certain personal issues involving Timothy, including an exhortation to remain pure and advice for the care for his chronic stomach problems.

Chapter 6 begins with Paul addressing those Christians who lived "under the yoke of slavery." He reminds them that they should consider their masters worthy of respect so that God's name and Christian teaching will not be slandered.

Having begun by addressing the poor and enslaved, Paul concludes by assigning Christian responsibilities to those who have prospered materially. They have been blessed by God in this way so that they can be a blessing to others, not so that they can indulge themselves and their own desires. They have a responsibility to be rich in good deeds and generosity, laying a foundation for the future so that they can take hold of the truly abundant life right now—not abundant in material possession but abundant in the things of God (see 1 Tim. 6:18–19).

> **They have been blessed by God in this way so that they can be a blessing to others.**

In closing, Paul entrusts to Timothy a word of warning to be delivered to those who trust in human knowledge:

Timothy, guard what has been entrusted to your care. Turn away from godless chatter and the opposing ideas of what is falsely called knowledge, which some have professed and in so doing have wandered from the faith.
Grace be with you (6:20–21).

Paul's first letter to Timothy is a letter for our own times, our own churches. It provides an objective standard against which to measure our modes of worship, church leaders, beliefs and doctrines, and cultural attitudes. In short, it offers clear and profound instructions from God in how to build a church. Truly, 1 Timothy is a letter for the twenty-first century as well as the first! God grant us eager, obedient hearts to read it, understand it, and live by it.

A Letter for Our Own Times

NOTES

NOTES

ADVENTURING
through
PAUL'S EPISTLES

CHAPTER TWELVE

2 TIMOTHY: STURDY CHRISTIANS *in a* COLLAPSING WORLD

I N A.D. 68, AN OLD MAN SITS in a filthy, rock-walled, circular cell in a Roman prison. This man, who once traveled the world telling thousands of people how to find an intimate relationship with the Creator of the universe, is now confined in a dingy space about twenty feet in diameter. From that prison cell, he writes a letter to a young man far across the Aegean and Adriatic Seas in the city of Ephesus. The subject of his letter: How to remain strong in the midst of a collapsing civilization.

In his second letter to Timothy, his son in the faith, Paul writes to a young man who is troubled by a weak constitution (a weak stomach, to be exact), a fearful spirit, and a timid outlook on life. And Timothy has much to be fearful about! Roman society in the first century is in rapid decline. The world is in political crisis and social chaos, and Timothy is surrounded by intense persecution. His friend and mentor Paul is in prison for his faith, facing a death sentence.

Paul knows that he will soon be with the Lord, and he wants to pass the torch to this younger man. He does so in this letter, which, in fact, is the last letter we have from Paul's pen. This is his farewell message, his final words of exhortation and friendship, his legacy, his last will and testament.

The Substance and Outline of 2 Timothy

In developing the theme of his second letter to Timothy—how to remain strong in the midst of a collapsing civilization—Paul focuses on four challenges that he wants to communicate to his young son in the faith.

Four
Challenges

1. Guard the truth.
2. Be strong in the Lord.
3. Avoid the traps and pitfalls of life.
4. Preach the Word.

These timeless challenges apply to today's Christians as well, and if I were to write to a young person today, I am sure I could never find anything better to say. Here is a structural overview of this letter:

A Christian's Responsibility in a Collapsing World (2 Timothy 1–2)

1.	Paul expresses thanks for Timothy's faith	1:1–5
2.	Timothy's responsibility as a pastor	1:6–18

3. The job description of a faithful pastor   2
    A. Teacher-discipler   2:1–2
    B. Soldier of God   2:3–4
    C. Athlete who competes by the rules   2:5
    D. Patient, hardworking farmer   2:6–13
    E. Diligent worker   2:14–19
    F. Instrument for God's use   2:20–23
    G. Gentle servant-teacher   2:24–26

The Christian's Strength in a Collapsing World (2 Timothy 3–4)

4. The coming time of apostasy   3
5. Preach the Word   4:1–5
6. Paul approaches the end of his life;   4:6–22
    parting words

Guard the Truth

Paul begins by reminding Timothy that God has given him a deposit of truth, which is his responsibility to guard:

> *Guard the good deposit that was entrusted to you—guard it with the help of the Holy Spirit who lives in us (2 Tim. 1:14).*

Paul then suggests certain ways to carry out this commission. Timothy lived in a pagan, secularized society, and Paul impressed upon him his responsibility to strengthen the defenses of the Ephesian church, which was imperiled by the pressures, temptations, and persecutions of the evil society around it.

While this letter is addressed to someone who is a pastor, Paul's challenge should be taken to heart by all Christians. Like Timothy, we have been given this same deposit of truth, this same fundamental revelation of the Scripture concerning the nature of reality: what the world is like, what God is like, what people are like, and what we need to do in order to be saved from our sin condition. From Timothy's day until now, people have wondered: *What makes the world operate the way it does? Why does it fall apart all the time? Why does nothing good seem to prosper and everything evil seem to reign unchallenged?* The answers are found in the deposit of truth that has been given to us through Jesus Christ, and we must guard it. Paul suggests three specific ways to do this:

> **Paul's challenge should be taken to heart by all Christians.**

- Guard the truth by exercising the spiritual gift God has given you.
- Guard the truth by suffering patiently.
- Guard the truth by following the pattern of sound teaching (read and trust the Scriptures).

Exercise Your
Spiritual Gifts

Paul addresses the first of these ways to guard the truth in 2 Timothy 1:6–7:

> *I remind you to fan into flame the gift of God, which is in you through the laying on of my hands. For God did not give us a spirit of timidity, but a spirit of power, of love and of self-discipline [or a sound mind].*

Over the years, my parishioners have come to me during various world crises and asked: What is going to happen in the world? What does it mean that communism has collapsed and the Berlin Wall has fallen? What does it mean that America is getting involved in a war in the Persian Gulf? What is going on in the Middle East? What is going on in Russia? What is going to happen at election time? Though I've studied Bible prophecy, I have no crystal ball (nor would I want one!). I don't think it's either useful or wise to try to match this or that headline with this or that specific verse in Scripture. We definitely see that the pattern of history and current events matches the pattern of prophecy, but I don't know how this event or that election fits into God's eternal plan.

As someone has wisely said, we don't know what the future holds, but we know who holds the future. Even more importantly, we know that God has not given us a spirit of timidity and fear. If we are anxious and troubled about what is going on in our nation and in the world, this fear and uncertainty does not come from God. The Spirit of God is the Spirit of power who prepares us for action. He is the Spirit of love who enables us to respond to people in a way that produces healing and grace. He is the Spirit of a sound mind who enables us to be intelligently purposeful in all we do. The way to discover this Spirit is to exercise the spiritual gifts that God has given us.

If you are a Christian, the indwelling Holy Spirit has given you a special ability. If you are not putting that spiritual gift to work, you are wasting your life. In the judgment of God—truly the only judgment that counts—all you accomplish outside of His will and His strength will be counted as so much wood, hay, and stubble, fit only to be burned.

What work has God given you to do? What spiritual gifts has He given you? Do you know? Have you discovered your purpose in life? Do you know what to look for? Do you know how to find it? When you have discovered your gifts and you begin to use them for His purpose, you will find that God does not give a spirit of fear but of power and love and a sound mind. That is Paul's first word to Timothy about how to guard the truth.

You might ask, "How does that work? How can using my spiritual gifts help to guard the truth?" It's simple: When you exercise your spiritual gifts, you literally unleash the truth and set it free to work in the world. The truth is not some fragile, brittle thing; rather, it is powerful, robust, vigorous, active. And the most effective way to guard God's truth is to unleash it in the world!

> When you exercise your spiritual gifts, you unleash the truth and set it free to work in the world.

Charles Spurgeon was exactly right when he said, "Truth is like a lion. Whoever heard of defending a lion? Turn it loose and it will defend itself." That is what we need to do with this truth. We do not need to apologize for it with theological, exegetical arguments. We do not need to fend off attacks on the truth. We merely need to set the truth free in the world, act on it, live it, use our spiritual gifts, and the truth will take care of itself!

The second way Paul says that we should guard the truth is by suffering patiently. He reminds Timothy that every Christian, without exception, is called to suffer for the gospel's sake.

Suffer Patiently

> *Do not be ashamed to testify about our Lord, or ashamed of me his prisoner. But join with me in suffering for the gospel, by the power of God (1:8).*

Later in this same letter, Paul makes a related statement:

> *In fact, everyone who wants to live a godly life in Christ Jesus will be persecuted (3:12).*

Many believers around the world suffer persecution and peril as a normal condition of being a Christian. More Christians were tortured and put to death for Christ's sake in the twentieth century than in any other, and worldwide trends indicate that the twenty-first century will likely be far worse, with increasing hostility toward those who follow Christ. The suffering that we will face, however, is not always physical; it can also be mental and emotional. This is the kind of suffering we endure when our faith is ridiculed, when we are excluded because of our moral and spiritual stand, when we are treated with open contempt or disdain, when our values and Christian lifestyles are mocked, laughed at, and derided. These are all forms of suffering for the gospel, and we are to accept this suffering with patience, says Paul. When we do so, we unleash the truth of God in the world, and without even defending ourselves, we guard the truth of God.

One of the reasons that the gospel is not widely accepted in many places today is that Christians have been impatient in suffering. Instead of patiently withstanding the abuse of this world, we have either been offended and outraged by persecution or we have given in and gone along with the crowd to escape having to suffer for the Lord's sake. We cannot challenge the sin and corruption of the world without getting the world mad at us. Obviously, we don't go out of our way to offend people, but the truth alone will bring about offense and backlash enough. The Scriptures make it clear that God is able to use our patient suffering for His truth as a tool for expanding the influence of His truth in the world. Our patient suffering is a potent, powerful way of guarding the truth of God.

> **God is able to use our patient suffering for His truth as a tool for expanding the influence of His truth in the world.**

Read and Trust the Scriptures

The third way in which Paul says we guard the truth is contained in Paul's admonition to Timothy: "What you heard from me, keep as the pattern of sound teaching" (1:13). In other words: Listen to, trust, and live out the Word of God.

I love that phrase, "the pattern of sound teaching." There are so many today who are departing from the pattern of sound teaching. They believe that some secular writer, out of the blindness and darkness of his or her own heart, has more insight into the problems of life than Scripture does. Yet when they repeat these arguments, or live according to this philosophy, they soon find themselves engulfed in neuroses, psychoses, and other problems, and they can't understand why. If we live as Paul tells Timothy he should live—guarding the truth that God has entrusted to us by exercising our gifts, suffering patiently, and trusting the Scriptures—God will guard us, protect us, and keep us secure in the faith, even amid this crumbling, collapsing world.

Be Strong in the Lord

Paul's second exhortation is: "Be strong in the Lord" (2:2). You never tell someone to be strong unless that person is capable of carrying it out. Obviously, Paul knew that Timothy had the capacity for strength—and you and I do as well. This is not a strength that we manufacture within ourselves but a strength that comes from trusting in the infinite power of Jesus Christ. There is a saying, "When I try, I fail. When I trust, He succeeds." Not I. He. His strength, remember, is perfected in our weakness (see 2 Cor. 12:9–10). That is the central truth about how the Christian life is to be lived.

Paul uses a number of word pictures to describe what it means to be strong in the Lord. First, we are to be strong as a soldier is strong; that is, we are to be utterly dedicated to the task. Second, we are to be strong as an athlete is strong; that is, we are to be disciplined and we are to abide by the rules of the Christian life so that we can compete to the utmost. Third, we are to be strong as a farmer is strong; that is, we are to be diligent in our work, not slowing down or slacking off, because we know that only if we work hard planting and cultivating will we be able to harvest. Dedication, discipline, and diligence—these are the keys to strength as described by Paul in this visual job description of the Christian.

> Dedication, discipline, and diligence are the keys to strength—the job description of the Christian.

He closes this second challenge with a reminder of the strength of the Lord. We are not merely to be strong, but to be strong *in the Lord*. He writes:

> *Remember Jesus Christ, raised from the dead, descended from David. This is my gospel (2:8).*

Paul wants Timothy to remember two things about Jesus: (1) He is the risen Christ, the Messiah, alive and powerful to be with us, completely unlimited by the constraints of space and time; (2) He is a human Christ, the Son of David, the one who has been where we are and who has felt what we feel—our pressures, our fears, our temptations, and our pain. He is the Son of God and the Son of Man, and He is the source of our strength in a crumbling, collapsing world.

Avoid the Traps and Pitfalls of Life

Paul's next challenge is found in 2:14–3:17. Here, he tells us to avoid the traps and pitfalls that lie in wait for us along the Christian life. He then describes some of those traps.

The first trap: battles over words. Have you ever noticed the way Christians often get upset over some little word in Scripture? Or over, say, a particular mode of baptism, or the exact timing of the Millennium? I've seen it many times—Christians dividing up into camps and choosing up weapons and battling it out. Paul says we must avoid this kind of conflict over words. These are stupid and useless controversies, dividing Christian from Christian, and they spread like gangrene. I'm not saying that such matters as baptism and the Millennium are unimportant; these are clearly areas of important biblical and scholarly inquiry, and Christians may engage in a robust discussion of such issues. But Christians should never separate over such issues.

The second trap: dangerous passions and temptations. Here is a word to a young man who must have felt the urgings of a normal sex drive and who lived in a sex-saturated society much like ours.

> *In a large house there are articles not only of gold and silver, but also of wood and clay; some are for noble purposes and some for ignoble. If a man cleanses himself from the latter, he will be an instrument for noble purposes, made holy, useful to the Master and prepared to do any good work (2:20–21).*

Paul uses a beautiful word picture here, depicting the whole world as a great house. In that house are instruments or vessels, representing people, and God uses these different instruments or vessels for either noble purposes or ignoble purposes. In other words, some people are like beautiful vases and crystal goblets. Others are like brick doorstops and brass spittoons. One way or another, God will use us for His purposes. It is completely up to us what kind of vessel we choose to be. God uses committed Christians to tell the world about His love, to draw others to faith in Him, to actively care for the hurting and the needy. But He also uses ungodly people.

Some years ago, a young man and a young woman were living together, unmarried, living a completely hedonistic lifestyle involving drug abuse. The young woman reached a point where she realized she was unhappy with her life, and she told the young man, "I don't know what it is, but I'm unhappy all the time." He replied, "I know what your problem is. If you want to be happy, you should ask Jesus Christ to come into your life. I know, because I was raised in a Christian home." When the woman asked why he didn't live according to Christian principles, he replied, "I want to live my life without rules, without morality. So I want nothing to do with Jesus. But if you really want to be happy, that's what you have to do." And the young woman accepted Christ, broke up with the young man, moved out, got involved in a church, and got her life straightened out. She became a noble vessel, willing to be used by God. He was an ignoble vessel, unwilling, but was used by God nonetheless!

Our goal as Christians is to be our best, most noble, most beautiful vessels for God. To be used for a noble purpose rather than ignoble, says Paul, we must separate ourselves from the things that would destroy our lives:

> *Flee the evil desires of youth, and pursue righteousness, faith, love and peace, along with those who call on the Lord out of a pure heart (2:22).*

One of the great destructive forces of our time is sexual immorality. Deadly sexually transmitted diseases, such as AIDS, are only the most visible harm this behavior causes. Sexual promiscuity destroys families, wounds the emotions and the psyches of men, women, and adolescents, and tears apart the very fabric of our civilization. Most people in our society seem to be blinded to this fact. But Christians have been instructed and warned: Flee evil desires, pursue purity before God. Then He will be able to use you for noble purposes, not ignoble.

The third trap: a rebellious attitude.

Avoid Lawless People

> *Mark this: There will be terrible times in the last days. People will be lovers of themselves, lovers of money, boastful, proud, abusive, disobedient to their parents, ungrateful, unholy, without love, unforgiving, slanderous, without self-control, brutal, not lovers of the good, treacherous, rash, conceited, lovers of pleasure rather than lovers of God—having a form of godliness but denying its power. Have nothing to do with them (3:1–5).*

First, understand that the phrase "last days" refers to the final end time of the church on earth. It includes the entire period of time between the first and the second comings of Christ. From the very day that our Lord rose from the dead, we have been in the last days. During these last days in which we now live, says Paul, there will come recurrent cycles of distress.

We are experiencing such times right now when people long for peace but are beset with anxiety about the future. Demonic forces are at work in the world, stirring up divisions, wars, racial strife, intergenerational tension, and even unprecedented warfare between men and women. Today we see characteristics that Paul describes: self-centeredness, greed, arrogance and pride, abuse, disobedience, and disrespect. These are characteristics of rebellion—an attitude of lawlessness. People—even Christians—can easily assume such an attitude. Paul says, "Avoid such people. Do not join them in their lawlessness."

Paul then shows Timothy the twofold way out of all these snares: (1) patience in suffering, and (2) persistence in truth (see 3:10 ff.).

"Remember the way I behaved," he says to Timothy. "You've seen how I've endured all the trials that came my way. Remember that if you're quietly patient in suffering and continue in the truth holding to the Scriptures and to what God has said, you will find your way safely through all the perils and the pitfalls of the collapsing world."

Preach the Word

In chapter 4, Paul gives Timothy his final challenge:

> *In the presence of God and of Christ Jesus, who will judge the living and the dead, and in view of his appearing and his kingdom, I give you this charge: Preach the Word; be prepared in season and out of season; correct, rebuke and encourage—with great patience and careful instruction (4:1–2).*

> **Correct, rebuke, and encourage all who will listen to the truth, in order to counteract the corrupting influence of this dying age.**

In other words, do not merely believe the Word but share it with others. Declare the great truth that God has given you. And there are three dimensions to declaring God's truth: Correct, rebuke, and encourage all who will listen to the truth, in order to counteract the corrupting influence of this dying age. For, as Paul adds in verse 3, a time is coming when people will not endure sound teaching.

Paul's Parting Words

Paul closes this commanding letter on a personal, poignant, yet triumphant note:

> *I am already being poured out like a drink offering, and the time has come for my departure. I have fought the good fight, I have*

*finished the race, I have kept the faith. Now there is in store for
me the crown of righteousness, which the Lord, the righteous Judge,
will award to me on that day—and not only to me, but also to all
who have longed for his appearing (4:6–8).*

That triumphant statement is all the more astounding when you remember the setting in which it was written. The apostle was imprisoned in a small stone-walled cell, cramped and cold, writing in semidarkness by the light of a sputtering oil lamp. He knew his fate was sealed. He had already been brought before Nero, that monster in human flesh, and he must appear before the Roman emperor once more. He knew how evil Nero was. Paul fully expected to be taken outside the city wall and, with a flash of the sword, to be beheaded.

But notice where Paul's gaze was fixed—not upon the moment of his death, but beyond death, to the crown of righteousness that awaited him. Death is but an incident to one who truly believes. Beyond death, victory beckons.

Yet, mingled with this passionate shout of triumph, we hear a chord of strong human emotion—especially the emotion of loneliness:

*Only Luke is with me. Get Mark and bring him with you, because
he is helpful to me in my ministry. I sent Tychicus to Ephesus.
When you come, bring the cloak that I left with Carpus at Troas,
and my scrolls, especially the parchments (4:11–13).*

Although Paul could look beyond his present circumstance to the glory of God that awaited him, see how human he is. This is normal. This is acceptable to God, because He knows what we are made of. He knows that it is difficult for a human being to remain hopeful when feeling lonely, cold, isolated, and bored. We can admit these feelings to God, and He fully accepts these feelings. There is nothing sinful about normal human emotion in times of trial.

> "There is nothing sinful about normal human emotion in times of trial."

Still, Paul's only concern at that moment was that he be able to proclaim God's message boldly and fully:

*At my first defense, no one came to my support, but everyone
deserted me. May it not be held against them. But the Lord stood
at my side and gave me strength, so that through me the message*

might be fully proclaimed and all the Gentiles might hear it. And I was delivered from the lion's mouth. The Lord will rescue me from every evil attack and will bring me safely to his heavenly kingdom. To him be glory for ever and ever. Amen (4:16–18).

Just as an aside, I have often thought about Paul's appearance before Nero. At that time, the name of Nero was honored and praised throughout the known world. He was the all-powerful emperor of the mighty Roman Empire. Who was Paul of Tarsus? A bald-headed, bowlegged man with weak eyes, poor speech, and a strange faith in a crucified Jew. Yet two thousand years later, the tables have been turned. Today, people name their sons Paul—and their dogs Nero.

Paul closes his letter to Timothy with a few personal words to his friends, familiar names like Priscilla and Aquila, and some lesser known names as well.

What a powerful letter this is, and how young Timothy's heart and life must have been affected by it. I would love to have gotten a letter like that from the apostle Paul, wouldn't you? Yet, in a real sense, that's exactly what this letter is: a letter to you and to me from the heart of Paul—and from the heart of God. Paul and God want us to know how to stand firm and be strong, even though the world seems to be collapsing all around us. No matter how bad this sorry world gets, we know that God enables us to be faithful in a world that is false, for He has not given us a spirit of timidity and fear, but of power, of love, and of a sound mind.

NOTES

NOTES

NOTES

Adventuring *through* Paul's Epistles

CHAPTER THIRTEEN

Titus: Hope *for the* Future, Help *for* Today

ALVIN TOFFLER'S BESTSELLER *Future Shock* describes the kind of stunned emotional reaction that people experience as the world changes all too rapidly around them. People experience "future shock" as they begin to see the future become a reality that is moving at the speed of light, leaving them behind. Amazingly, the future shock of which Toffler wrote in the early 1970s did begin to take into account our present age of personal computers, Stealth fighters and cruise missiles, the Internet, cellular phones, the demise of communism, and so much more.

Our world has changed—and continues to change—even faster than a futurist like Toffler could have imagined. As a result, many people have given up on the future and have settled into a state of despair. But in Paul's letter to Titus, we find a powerful antidote to future shock. Paul calls this antidote "our blessed hope." Even though the world is changing, even though our heads are spinning as we try to keep up with the dizzying pace of new developments in our society, we have a hope that anchors our future and enables us to feel secure . . .

> Jesus will appear in glory to set right all the things that are wrong in this world. That is our hope.

while we wait for the blessed hope—the glorious appearing of our great God and Savior, Jesus Christ (Titus 2:13).

Jesus will appear in glory to set right all the things that are wrong in this world. That is our hope. That is the cure for our future shock. That is one of the themes that Paul weaves into his letter to Titus.

The Background and Structure of Titus

Titus was one of the young men who accompanied the apostle Paul on many of his missionary journeys. Titus was a Greek who came to Christ in the city of Antioch. At the time this letter was written, he was on the island of Crete, just south of Greece.

The church in Crete likely was begun by Paul and Titus after Paul's first imprisonment in Rome. Apparently, Paul was released from that imprisonment, as recorded in the book of Acts. You may recall that Paul had expressed the desire to go to Spain, and many scholars believe that after his journey to Spain, he and Titus went to the island of Crete and began the church there. According to this letter, he left Titus there to "straighten out what was left unfinished and appoint elders in every town, as I [Paul] directed you" (1:5). This letter provides interesting insight into what occurred in the early church as Paul traveled and sent these young men as apostolic delegates to do special work for him in various places.

Paul's letter to Titus is short and practical, rich in instruction and encouragement. Its themes are interwoven throughout, so we will explore it theme by theme. Thus, we may seem to jump from, say, chapter 3 to chapter 1 and back again, but I believe that you will find this method to be a helpful way to examine the truths of this book. Here is an overview of the structure of Paul's letter to Titus:

> *Titus is short and practical, rich in instruction and encouragement.*

Church Leadership (Titus 1)

1.	Introductory remarks	1:1–4
2.	The qualifications of elders (church leaders)	1:5–9
3.	Dealing with false teachers in the church	1:10–16

Christian Living in Difficult Times (Titus 2–3)

4.	Teach sound doctrine	2
5.	Commit to good works	3:1–11
6.	Conclusion	3:12–15

The Character of the Cretans

In one of the most unusual passages in the New Testament, Paul quotes from one of the ancient writers of his day, a secular Greek poet who characterized the people of Crete, among whom young Titus lived and labored:

> *Even one of their own prophets has said, "Cretans are always liars, evil brutes, lazy gluttons" (1:12).*

It is obvious that Paul wants Titus, his son in the faith, to understand the formidable problem that he is facing. Paul warns him that he is dealing with dishonest, brutish, lazy, and gluttonous people. He underscores this by adding, "This testimony is true" (v. 13). As we move through the letter, Paul amplifies and explores these characteristics of the Cretan people. For example, Paul says,

> *To the pure, all things are pure, but to those who are corrupted and do not believe, nothing is pure. In fact, both their minds and consciences are corrupted. They claim to know God, but by their*

actions they deny him. They are detestable, disobedient and unfit for doing anything good (1:15–16).

This was the kind of wicked society in which the Cretan church existed. The minds and consciences of the people were corrupted. They professed to know God, yet they denied Him by their deeds and by their attitudes toward one another. He amplifies this theme in chapter 3:

Avoid foolish controversies and genealogies and arguments and quarrels about the law, because these are unprofitable and useless. Warn a divisive person once, and then warn him a second time. After that, have nothing to do with him. You may be sure that such a man is warped and sinful; he is self-condemned (vv. 9–11).

> When the church is beset with problems, it is usually because the world is invading the church, not because the church is invading the world!

These words refer primarily to those who profess to be Christian but whose lives reflect the attitudes of the evil world around them. The purpose of the church is to invade the world with the love of Jesus Christ. When the church is beset with problems, it is usually because the world is invading the church, not because the church is invading the world! The gospel is a disturbing element in the world, and whenever the church is true to its authentic message, it becomes a revolutionary body. The revolution it brings is one of love and purity that challenges the wicked, brutish status quo.

Sound Doctrine and Good Deeds

In chapter 3, Paul speaks not only of Cretans, but also of himself and of all human beings as we were before becoming Christians. Here is a description of the world as God sees it:

At one time we too were foolish, disobedient, deceived and enslaved by all kinds of passions and pleasures. We lived in malice and envy, being hated and hating one another (v. 3).

This is the kind of world into which the apostle Paul sent young Titus with the power of the gospel.

What did these people need? Several times throughout this letter, we read the phrase "sound doctrine." Paul knew that in order to change society, people must be told the truth. People walk in darkness and act like animals, tearing one another apart and hating one another, for one of two reasons: Either they have rejected the truth, or they have never heard the truth. So *begin by teaching them the truth.*

Another basic need is "good deeds." This phrase appears five times in Titus. Chapter 1 ends with a description of those who are "unfit for doing anything good" (1:16). Chapter 2 says, "In everything set them an example by doing what is good" (2:7), and the chapter closes with the idea that Jesus gave Himself "to purify for himself a people that are his very own, eager to do what is good" (2:14). In chapter 3, Paul says, "those who have trusted in God [should] be careful to devote themselves to doing what is good" (v. 8), and adds that Christians "must learn to devote themselves to doing what is good" (v. 14). Sound doctrine alone is not enough. The world is looking for good deeds that back up our good doctrine.

> The world is looking for good deeds that back up our good doctrine.

We keep trying to change the way people are and the way they behave. We try to change people with education, or with tougher laws, or with inducements and rewards—but nothing works. People are people, and human nature is the same today as it ever was. As someone has well said, "If you bring a pig into the parlor, it won't change the pig, but it will certainly change the parlor!" And that is the problem. It's not enough to try to change people's behavior. Their very nature has to be transformed. That's what the truth of salvation is all about, and that is the truth Paul says is desperately needed—by all people in every era. In chapter 3, he says,

> *At one time we too were foolish, disobedient, deceived and enslaved*
> *by all kinds of passions and pleasures. We lived in malice and*
> *envy, being hated and hating one another. But when the kindness*
> *of God our Savior appeared, he saved us, not because of righteous*
> *things we had done, but because of his mercy. He saved us through*
> *the washing of rebirth and renewal by the Holy Spirit (3:3–5).*

Good deeds are not enough; our greatest need is not merely to become nicer people. We need to be turned inside out and shaken! We need to be completely changed! We need to be saved! That's what Paul means when he talks about "the washing of rebirth and renewal." God does not patch us up from the outside like an old inner tube; He completely makes us over from the inside. He melts us down and remolds us in His own image, by the washing of regeneration and renewal in the Holy Spirit. The supreme message of the church is to proclaim this great good news: "the hope of eternal life" (v. 7).

Hope: The Answer to Future Shock and Present Despair

When the Bible speaks of hope, it does not use the word in the same way we usually do, meaning a faint glimmer of a possibility: "I hope I win the Irish sweepstakes," or, "I hope that clattering sound in the engine doesn't mean what I think it does!" When the New Testament speaks of hope, it speaks of *certainty*. The hope of eternal life rests upon the One who came to give us eternal life, and we are justified by His grace. This is rock-solid reality!

> **When the New Testament speaks of hope, it speaks of certainty.**

Here is our shock-proof hope for the future, our bullet-proof shield against the uncertainty of tomorrow. The world is changing rapidly. We witness morality crumbling, deviant behavior being called normal, moral values being redefined as "repressive." We see good being called evil, and evil, good. Arrogance, extremism, and hedonism are celebrated and applauded in our society; humility, moderation, and virtue are ridiculed. If we do not have a rock-solid hope in the midst of such rapidly shifting, dizzying, sickening changes, we will succumb to despair. Paul describes the hope that God has given us in Titus 2:11–13:

> *The grace of God that brings salvation has appeared to all men. It teaches us to say "No" to ungodliness and worldly passions, and to live self-controlled, upright and godly lives in this present age, while we wait for the blessed hope—the glorious appearing of our great God and Savior, Jesus Christ.*

This is the answer to future shock and present despair—our blessed hope, the glorious appearing of our great God and Savior, Jesus Christ.

In this passage Paul clearly identifies Jesus as *God*. Many people today try to escape this truth of Scripture, but we see it clearly stated throughout the gospel of John, in Philippians 2, and in Titus 2:13. And wherever it is not stated with such unambiguous, obvious clarity as we see here, it is always implied throughout the Old and New Testaments: Jesus the Messiah is the eternal God in human flesh.

Qualifications for Leadership

Another major issue that Paul addresses in his letter to Titus is church leadership. The Cretans needed to understand how an orderly Christian church should function, so in the opening chapter he describes the qualifications for church leaders (the word *elder* refers to the individual holding the leadership office; the word *bishop* refers to the office itself).

> *An elder must be blameless, the husband of but one wife, a man whose children believe and are not open to the charge of being wild and disobedient. Since an overseer is entrusted with God's work, he must be blameless—not overbearing, not quick-tempered, not given to drunkenness, not violent, not pursuing dishonest gain. Rather he must be hospitable, one who loves what is good, who is self-controlled, upright, holy and disciplined (1:6–8).*

Where do you find such people? Paul expected Titus to find them in Crete. He expected God to raise up people of proven character, faith, and spiritual gifts from among those who had once been characterized as liars, evil brutes, and lazy gluttons. The gospel effects such transformation. Properly understood, the church is a community of change, a family in which God's grace and the love of His people bring about radical healing, therapy, and redirection. That is what a church is created to accomplish.

> The church is a community of change.

Paul also tells Titus that he needs to teach the Christians in Crete about civic responsibility:

> *Remind the people to be subject to rulers and authorities, to be obedient, to be ready to do whatever is good, to slander no one, to be peaceable and considerate, and to show true humility toward all men (3:1–2).*

Paul exhorts the church to recognize that the authorities are in a real sense God's ministers (whether or not they see themselves and offer themselves to God as such). God has ordained government to maintain order in human society, so we should be respectful and obedient to the law in every area except those in which government opposes God's law.

How practical this letter is! And how relevant to our own lives today! As Paul gives these guidelines, he is quietly injecting into the Cretan community a power that, if followed, would transform the national character of Crete, just as it will transform the national character of our own society.

Words of Admonition and Advice

Paul closes his letter to Titus with personal words of admonition and advice, giving us a penetrating glimpse into his own life.

> *As soon as I send Artemas or Tychicus to you, do your best to come to me at Nicopolis, because I have decided to winter there (3:12).*

Nicopolis was on the western shore of Greece, just across the Adriatic Sea from the heel of the Italian boot. Paul, probably writing from Corinth in Greece, was sending two young men down to replace Titus in Crete, so that Titus could rejoin Paul. Later we read that Titus went on up to Dalmatia, on the northern coast, sending Zenas, the lawyer, and Apollos on their way (perhaps to Alexandria, which was Apollos' home), and Paul admonishes Titus to make sure that they lack nothing.

Paul closes the letter by bringing it full circle with the opening verse. He began the letter with this statement:

> *Paul, a servant of God and an apostle of Jesus Christ for the faith of God's elect* and the knowledge of the truth that leads to godliness *(1:1, emphasis added).*

He closes with these words:

> *Our people* must learn to devote themselves to doing what is good, *in order that they may provide for daily necessities and not live unproductive lives.*
> *Everyone with me sends you greetings. Greet those who love us in the faith.*
> *Grace be with you all (3:14–15, emphasis added).*

Truth leads to godliness. Sound doctrine and good deeds go hand in hand. We must know the truth—and then we must do it. The basis of the truth of the gospel that transforms our lives and our behavior is, as Paul says in Titus 1:2, "the hope of eternal life, which God, who does not lie, promised before the beginning of time."

> **We are living out our eternal lives right now.**

The promise that Paul talks about is found in Genesis, where God promised before Adam and Eve were driven out of Eden that a Redeemer would come and bring life to humanity (see Gen. 3:15). That Redeemer has come;

His name is Jesus. That hope is now—not just the expectation of heaven, but the strength for living in these troubled times. We are living out our eternal lives right now, today, as we live in reliance upon Him.

NOTES

NOTES

ADVENTURING
through
PAUL'S EPISTLES

CHAPTER FOURTEEN

PHILEMON:
A BROTHER
RESTORED

CLARA BARTON, THE FOUNDER of the American Red Cross, was once painfully betrayed by a coworker. Years later, a friend reminded her of the incident. "I don't remember that," replied Miss Barton.

"You don't remember?" asked the astonished friend. "But you were so hurt at the time! Surely you must remember!"

"No," Clara Barton insisted gently. "I distinctly remember forgetting that ever happened."

As we are about to see in our adventure through Paul's letter to Philemon, this is the true nature of forgiveness: It's a deliberate decision to forget wrongs suffered.

> **Christlike forgiving grace is the strongest force in the universe.**

Christlike forgiving grace is the strongest force in the universe. It is the power to restore broken relationships, to heal shattered churches, to make families whole once more. It is the heart of the gospel. It is the key to the book of Philemon.

The Structure and Uniqueness of Philemon

The structure of this short, one-chapter book is very simple:

Paul's Appeal to Philemon (Philemon 1–25)

1. Paul gives thanks to God for his friend Philemon — 1–7
2. Paul asks Philemon to forgive Onesimus — 8–16
3. Paul's promise to Philemon — 17–21
4. Personal remarks, greetings from others, benediction — 22–25

This is the fourth of Paul's personal letters (following the two letters to Timothy and the letter to Titus), and it differs from all of Paul's other letters in that it contains no instruction that is intended for the church as a whole or as foundational doctrine. Instead, this is a letter that applies, in a powerful, practical way, all the tenets and values contained in Paul's other writings: love, acceptance, forgiveness, grace, and Christian brotherhood.

Philemon and Onesimus

The epistle to Philemon was written when the apostle Paul was a prisoner in the city of Rome for the first time. Philemon, who lived in the Greek city of Colossae, was a friend whom Paul had won to Christ, and he apparently had a young brother named Onesimus. Although many believe there was no blood relationship between Philemon and his slave, Onesimus, I am strongly convinced, because of what Paul says in verse 16, that they were brothers:

> [Receive him as] a brother beloved, specially to me, but how much more unto thee, both in the flesh, and in the Lord? (KJV)

What else could a brother "in the flesh" be but a brother by birth, a distinction Paul seems to underscore when he adds that Onesimus is also a Christian brother, a brother "in the Lord." This distinction is blurred in the NIV, which reads: "He is very dear to me but even dearer to you, both as a man and as a brother in the Lord." Although the NIV is an excellent translation, I believe the King James Version is more accurate at this point.

Given the view that Onesimus was Philemon's brother in the flesh, we find some powerful applications in this letter that we can use in relating to each other not only as Christians but within our families. As you probably know, one of the hardest places to apply lessons of love, acceptance, and forgiveness is at home, within our own family relationships. So many of us seem to have a huge blind spot in our closest relationships. We treat family members in ways we wouldn't think of treating even a rude stranger on the street.

> One of the hardest places to apply lessons of love, acceptance, and forgiveness is within our own family relationships.

I believe that what probably happened in the relationship between these two brothers, Onesimus and Philemon, is that Onesimus got into some sort of financial trouble. Perhaps he was a gambler, or perhaps some other issue in his life brought him into financial disgrace. In those days, people in financial trouble could not appeal to bankruptcy court to bail them out. But they could sometimes get someone to redeem them by selling themselves to that person as a slave.

Perhaps Onesimus got into debt and went to his brother, Philemon, and said, "Phil, would you help me? I'm in trouble and I need some cash."

Philemon might have said, "Well, Onesimus, what can you give me for security?" And Onesimus would have replied, "You know I haven't got a thing but myself, so I'll become your slave if you'll pay off this debt."

That may or may not have been how it occurred, but it is one likely scenario.

If irresponsibility got Onesimus into this jam in the first place, it is easy to see why he might choose to run away from his responsibilities to his brother. But whatever the situation was, we know that Onesimus fled and took refuge in Rome, where he apparently found Christ while under Paul's instruction, during Paul's first imprisonment there.

Masters and Slaves

Philemon may well have been a Christian for some time when this letter was written, for we know that in Colossians 4:9 he is commended as a faithful and beloved brother who had been of great service to Paul and to the gospel.

But why would a faithful Christian be a slave owner? This question naturally occurs to us because slavery seems so abhorrent to us today. Slavery, however, was an accepted part of the Roman culture. In Paul's other epistles we see several admonitions to believers who were slaves and masters.

To Slaves   *Slaves, obey your earthly masters with respect and fear, and with sincerity of heart, just as you would obey Christ. Obey them not only to win their favor when their eye is on you, but like slaves of Christ, doing the will of God from your heart (Eph. 6:5–6).*

Slaves, obey your earthly masters in everything; and do it, not only when their eye is on you and to win their favor, but with sincerity of heart and reverence for the Lord (Col. 3:22).

Teach slaves to be subject to their masters in everything, to try to please them, not to talk back to them (Titus 2:9).

To Masters   *Masters, treat your slaves in the same way. Do not threaten them, since you know that he who is both their Master and yours is in heaven, and there is no favoritism with him (Eph. 6:9).*

Masters, provide your slaves with what is right and fair, because you know that you also have a Master in heaven (Col. 4:1).

Ultimately, it would be Christian principles such as human equality, love, grace, and our Christian duties to one another that would break down cultural attitudes and end slavery. But that was in the future. In Paul's day, slavery was a reality that had to be dealt with. And even though slaves continued to serve their masters, he challenged both slaves and masters to see each other as kindred, and to worship together in the church on an equal footing—which must have been a startling concept to those around them.

> Paul challenged both slaves and masters to see each other as kindred, and to worship together in the church on an equal footing.

In the Roman Empire, a slave's life was usually harsh, cruel, and unforgiving. If a slave ran away from his master, he could either be put to death or shipped back to his master for punishment—and there were virtually no limits to the amount or severity of punishment and torture that could be applied.

When Onesimus ran away, he apparently compounded his problems by stealing money from Philemon. He found his way to Rome, was converted to Christ through Paul's ministry, and became an assistant to Paul. But Paul was determined to send him back to Philemon so that Onesimus could clear his conscience of all past transgressions. So, Paul wrote this gracious little note and sent it to Philemon in the hand of Onesimus himself.

The Return of Onesimus

Imagine the scene at Philemon's home when this letter arrives. Philemon stands on his porch one morning looking down the road, and he sees someone approaching. He says to his wife, Apphia, "Doesn't that look like my ne'er-do-well runaway brother?"

Sure enough, it's Onesimus himself. The black sheep has returned. Anger floods through Philemon, and as Onesimus comes within earshot, he growls, "So you've come home at last! What brings you back?"

Without a word of defense, Onesimus hands his brother a scroll. Philemon takes it and reads:

> *Paul, a prisoner of Christ Jesus, and Timothy our brother,*
>   *To Philemon our dear friend and fellow worker, to Apphia our sister, to Archippus our fellow soldier and to the church that meets in your home:*
>   *Grace to you and peace from God our Father and the Lord Jesus Christ (vv. 1–3).*

"This is from Paul," Philemon says to his wife, "That's the way he always begins his letters. I don't know how my brother got this letter, but it is authentic."

Note the reference in these opening verses: "and to the church that meets in your home." Believers gathered together in Philemon's home to study and pray together. This is the church that Paul greets. Not a building of stone walls, stained glass, and wooden pews, but people gathered in Philemon's home to study God's Word, to pray together, and to share their struggles and their strength.

Philemon goes on reading:

> *I always thank my God as I remember you in my prayers, because I hear about your faith in the Lord Jesus and your love for all the saints. I pray that you may be active in sharing your faith, so that you will have a full understanding of every good thing we have in Christ (vv. 4–6).*

Philemon says, "Imagine, Paul has been praying for us, even from prison. Isn't that amazing?" He reads on, and sees the first indication of why Paul is writing to him:

> *Although in Christ I could be bold and order you to do what you ought to do, yet I appeal to you on the basis of love. I then, as Paul—an old man and now also a prisoner of Christ Jesus—I appeal to you for my son Onesimus, who became my son while I was in chains (vv. 8–10).*

Paul says, in effect, "I could order you to do this by my authority as an apostle, but instead I will appeal to you on the basis of your own Christlike love." He then goes on to describe Onesimus as one "who became my son while I was in chains." I think the tears probably came to Philemon's eyes as he read this. Here was dear old Paul, who had led him to Christ, sitting in that lonely prison, writing, "Philemon, old friend, would you do me a favor? I'm appealing to you, even though I could command you. I'd appreciate a special favor from you while I am here in prison." How could Philemon's heart not melt at these words?

I imagine Philemon turning to his wife and saying, "Look! It says here that Paul, the apostle who led me to the Lord, has had the same influence on my brother and slave, Onesimus. Not only do we have the same father in the flesh, but now Paul is a spiritual father to us both!"

In the next verse, we encounter an interesting play on words:

Formerly he was useless to you, but now he has become useful both to you and to me (v. 11).

Clearly, Onesimus was worse than useless to Philemon. He'd stolen from Philemon and run away. Useless? He was a nuisance! He was trouble! He was bad news! And what is truly ironic is that the name Onesimus literally means "useful" or "profitable."

Paul has a wonderful sense of humor and enjoys a well-aimed pun now and then, as he does here, saying, in effect, "Mr. Useful may have been Mr. Useless to you once, but he's now Mr. Useful once more!" And so, as he adds in verse 12, he is sending Mr. Useful back to Philemon, where he can live in a way that is worthy of his name.

He sends Onesimus, in fact, because Paul views Onesimus' service to Philemon as service to himself. Although Paul would like to keep this useful young man with him, he would much rather see Onesimus repay his debt to Philemon, whom he has wronged.

Slaves of One Master

The key to this little letter is in the sixteenth verse, where Paul tells Philemon that he is sending Onesimus back to him . . .

no longer as a slave, but better than a slave, as a dear brother. He is very dear to me but even dearer to you, both as a man [or, brother in the flesh] and as a brother in the Lord.

With these words, Paul erases the line of distinction between slave and free. The rigid boundaries of cultural views are transcended by love and kinship in Christ. Regardless of position—slave or master, according to Roman customs—both are slaves of one Master, Jesus Christ. This also must be our view as we approach the people around us. Instead of labeling others according to economic status, political views, race, or any other characteristic, we must begin to see them as people for whom Christ died, people of whom Christ is Lord.

As he reads Paul's letter, Philemon's heart begins to turn toward his black sheep brother. I can imagine him saying to his wife, "If Paul found Onesimus so dear to him, maybe we ought to forgive him for all the things he has done. Maybe the fellow has been changed. Let's see what else Paul has to say." And he reads verse 17:

If you consider me a partner, welcome him as you would welcome me.

"Well," Philemon might have said, "this puts quite a different slant on things. I was going to take Onesimus back—as a slave! I was going to house him in the slave quarters and put him back to work. But Paul says I should receive Onesimus as if he were Paul himself!"

Apphia says, "Well, we surely would never send our brother Paul down to the slave house. We would give him the best guest room in the house. So if we are going to receive Onesimus as we would receive Paul, we'd better give him the best room."

Do you hear in this story an echo of the story of the loving father and the Prodigal Son (see Luke 15)?

So Philemon says, "All right. Let's get the guest room ready . . . but just a moment! Hold everything! Onesimus never paid back the money he took!"

But Paul addresses this issue, too. In verses 18 and 19, he writes,

If he has done you any wrong or owes you anything, charge it to me. I, Paul, am writing this with my own hand. I will pay it back—not to mention that you owe me your very self.

That is grace. That is the gospel. That is what God has done for us through Jesus Christ. The debt we owe has been paid by another. Here is the doctrine of acceptance and the doctrine of substitution wonderfully portrayed for us in a living object lesson. In fact, Martin Luther once observed, "All of us were God's Onesimus." We were slaves. We were debtors. We were sinners. We merited nothing. On our own, we stand naked and wretched before a God who is righteous and holy, yet the Lord Jesus says to the Father, "If this one has done anything wrong, or owes you anything, charge it to my account. I will pay it." That is what Paul says here.

> All of us were God's Onesimus.

The Far Reach of Grace

Philemon's heart must have been melted by this amazing expression of grace from Paul's heart as he wrote from the solitude of his cold prison cell. Paul had nothing—no money with which to repay the debt of Onesimus—yet he wrote, "If he owes you anything, put it on my tab. I'll pay it myself when I come."

That, I think, was the crowning touch of Paul's entire appeal. With that, I believe Philemon's heart broke, he opened his arms, hugged Onesimus to himself, and forgave him. The kinship of the family was restored once again.

Paul understood that the two brothers could not live together as fam- Broken Chains ily when one was a slave and one was a master. Both had to be free of the chains that bound them—Onesimus from the chains of his debt to Philemon and Philemon from the chains of his cultural blindness, which saw mastery over his brother Onesimus as his legal right. In the end, those chains were broken not by the force of law; they were dissolved by the free-flowing waters of love and grace.

As this brief letter draws to a close, Paul makes this affirming statement:

> *Confident of your obedience, I write to you, knowing that you will do even more than I ask (v. 21).*

Here we see how far grace can reach in affecting human lives, relationships, and behavior. Paul has appealed to Philemon on the basis of grace. If he had chosen instead to impose demands on Philemon on the basis of law, on the basis of his authority as an apostle, he would have said, "Philemon! As the holy apostle of the holy church, I command you to accept this young man back into your household and to give him back his job!" That is as far as law can go. And Philemon would have obeyed such a legal demand. But grace reaches so much farther than law. Grace not only restored Onesimus to his job in the household of Philemon, but restored him to a relationship, to a place of love and belonging in the family of Philemon! Grace breaks down all the barriers, smooths out the friction, cleanses the bitterness, and heals the pain of the past.

Grace breaks down all the barriers, smooths out the friction, cleanses the bitterness, and heals the pain of the past.

Paul then adds this request:

> *And one thing more: Prepare a guest room for me, because I hope to be restored to you in answer to your prayers (v. 22).*

From this statement it is clear that the apostle expects to be released from prison. But how? "I hope to be restored to you *in answer to your prayers*," he writes. And we know that God did indeed grant these requests.

Paul was released, and he preached the Word of God for several more years before he was incarcerated for the second time.

Finally, Paul sends greetings from some of those who were with him. Epaphras was well known in Colossae; he had founded the church there. But now as a fellow prisoner with Paul in Rome, he sends greetings, as does Mark, author of the gospel of Mark, and Aristarchus, one of Paul's disciples. Demas was a young man who later forsook Paul (as we discover in the last letter that Paul wrote) because "he loved this world" (2 Tim. 4:10). Luke, author of the gospel of Luke and the book of Acts, also was with Paul in Rome and sent greetings to Philemon.

Paul closes his letter to Philemon with words so characteristic of the apostle of grace:

The grace of the Lord Jesus Christ be with your spirit (v. 25).

Here is the theme of Philemon, the theme of the apostle Paul, the theme of the entire Word of God to human beings, who are lost in sin: Grace is the answer to all our problems, all our pain. It is the answer to our guilt and sin. It is the answer to our troubled relationships. It is the answer to our fear of death.

God's grace has been shed upon us through the Lord Jesus Christ. And His grace calls us to show the same Christlike quality of grace to those grace-starved souls around us, the Onesimus-like people we meet every day and especially those in our own homes.

May God give us grace to represent His gracious character every day.

NOTES

NOTES

NOTES

NOTE TO THE READER

The publisher invites you to share your response to the message of this book by writing Discovery House Publishers, P.O. Box 3566, Grand Rapids, MI 49501, U.S.A. For information about other Discovery House books, music, videos, or DVDs, contact us at the same address or call 1-800-653-8333. Find us on the Internet at *http://www.dhp.org/* or send e-mail to **books@dhp.org**.